orde's Conversations

with

Henry Moore

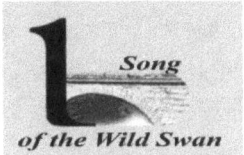

Song
of the Wild Swan

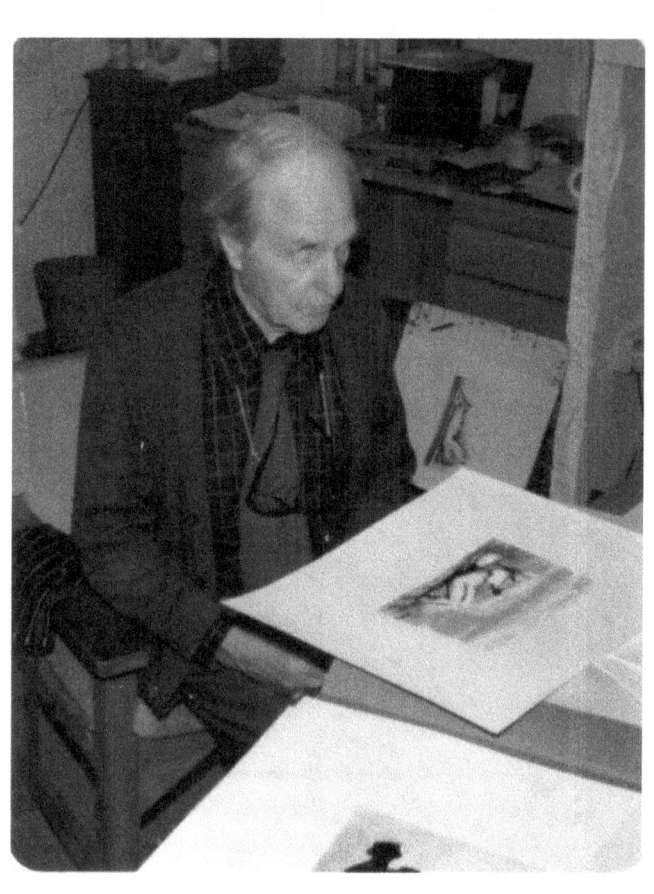

PUBLISHED
ON THE OCCASION OF THE ARTIST'S
80TH BIRTHDAY ON 30 JULY 1978

Published by Song, 2014.
Song is an Imprint of:
Song of the Wild Swan Ltd.
1 Folly Bridge, Oxford, OX1 4LB, UK.
www.songwildswan.com
tel +44 (0) 1865 240572
fax +44 (0) 1865 246565
e: info@songwildswan.com

orde's Conversations with Henry Moore
ISBN 9781909777163

First published: Unedited conversation, 1978 in hardback (75 copies) to accompany the Henry Moore 80th Anniversary Portfolio.
Edited conversations published in 1978 as softback (500 copies).
eBook and Book: Unedited and Edited, 2014 Song, Oxford.

Acknowledgements

Song eBook Design series by Laurence Hutton-Smith.
Cover Design, Laurence Hutton-Smith.
Cover Image: Atom Piece (Working Model for Nuclear Energy) 1964-5
(LH525), Henry Moore, Bronze. And nine print images including Woman
with Book, Woman with Arms Crossed, Woman with Clasped Hands,
Two Seated Figures against Pillar, Woman with Dove, Mother and Child
with Wave Background I, II and III, Reclining Figure with
Stormy Sky (CGM 442-450) 1976
© Henry Moore Foundation, 2014.
Reproduced by permission of The Henry Moore Foundation
Book Production: Amaury Marinho Junior

Contents

Foreword

This publication combines both the hardcover edition and the edited soft-cover of my conversations with Henry Moore at Much Hadham in 1978 when I published his *80th Anniversary Portfolio* of graphics. How it came about is set out in the introduction to the hardcover introduction reproduced in this publication and I see no need to change anything.

The softcover edition was primarily due to a request for an edited version using only Moore's words. As an exercise I found it does present a different picture both of Moore and myself.

I prefer to have the full text to give the full flavour of what was a great discussion rather than editing the words of others, especially as Moore felt no need for it either. I thought it would be interesting to have one publication with both versions so as not to ignore the past, and to allow comparisons and show how any editing does change sense and meaning. The paperback edition contained the same publication details (so it is not reproduced twice) but the introduction was changed, photographs of Moore were selected and printed in black and white (rather than colour) and the conversation was edited – so these are all reprinted as they were done originally.

One incident I do recall worth mentioning in regard to this publication is that I was questioned as to the appropriateness of including photographs I had taken of Moore which showed the holes in his jersey. When I asked Moore if he minded he simply replied: *'of course not, the jersey is an old friend'*.

Orde, Oxford, 24 November 2013.

Publication Details

The original Henry Moore 80th Anniversary Portfolio was published by orde on the occasion of the artist's 80th birthday on 30 July 1978. The portfolio was limited to forty numbered copies plus ten dedication copies. These dedication copies were allocated by the artist as follows:

Exhibition Copy
Complete Collection (Henry Moore Foundation Archive Copy)
Art Gallery of Ontario, Toronto
Tate Gallery, London
Victoria and Albert Museum, London
Wilhelm Lehnbruck Museum, Duisberg
and two others to remain for dedications.

Each portfolio contains nine original colour lithographs numbered and signed by Henry Moore, as well as a leather-bound book autographed by the artist. This book gives the text of a conversation with Henry Moore pertaining to these lithographs as well as photographs taken on that occasion. The lithographs are mounted and together with the book appear in a cloth-bound numbered portfolio.

Henry Moore editioned certain litographs to 40 and others to 50 – their allocation was as follows:

Nos. 1/50 to 40/50 inclusive of the following lithographs have been allocated to the portfolio:-Two Seated Figures against Pillar; Reclining Figure with Stormy Sky; Woman with Book; Woman with Arms Crossed; Woman with Dove and Woman with Clasped Hands.

Nos. 41/50 – 50/50 of the above lithographs are for sale individually.

Nos. 1/40 to 40/40 of the following lithographs have been allocated to the portfolio: Mother and Child with Wave Background I; Mother and Child with Wave Background II and Mother and Child with Wave Background III.

There are ten artist's proofs of all nine above-mentioned lithographs. Henry Moore has numbered them i/x to x/x.

The dedication copies mentioned in the preliminary pages are marked according to their allocation, thus the exhibition copy is marked E. C.; the Tate Gallery copy is marked for the Tate Gallery and so on.

Woman with Book 1976
Image Size 8 x 5½ ins. (20,32 x 13,97 cm)
Paper Size 18½ 14 ins. (47,00 x 35,56 cm)
5 colour Lithograph
Edition of 50 plus 10 artist's proofs
Paper: Hand made T. H. Saunders
Printer: Curwen Studio
Publisher: Orde Levinson Fine Art

Woman with Arms Crossed 1976
Image Size 6 x 7 1/8 ins. (15,24 x 18,10 cm)
Paper Size 1½x 14 ins. (47,00 x 35,56 cm)
4 colour Lithograph
Edition of 50 plus 10 artist's proofs
Paper: Hand made T. H. Saunders
Printer: Curwen Studio
Publisher: Orde Levinson Fine Art

Woman with Clasped Hands 1976
Image Size 51/8 x 7 ins. (13,02 x 17,78 cm)
Paper Size 18½ x 14 ins. (47,00 x 35,56 cm)
4 colour Lithograph
Edition of 50 plus 10 artist's proofs
Paper: Hand made T. H. Saunders
Printer: Curwen Studio
Publisher: Orde Levinson Fine Art

Two Seated Figures Against Pillar 1976
Image Size 5 3/8 x 9 ins. (13,65 x 22,86 cm)
Paper Size 18½ x 14 ins. (47,00 x 35,56 cm)
5 colour Lithograph
Edition of 50 plus 10 artist's proofs
Paper: Hand made T. H. Saunders
Printer: Curwen Studio
Publisher: Orde Levinson Fine Art

Woman with Dove 1976
Image Size 11 x 8¼ ins. (27,94 x 20,95 cm)
Paper Size 18½ x 14ins. (47,00 x 35,56 cm)
6 colour Lithograph
Edition of 50 plus 10 artist's proofs
Paper: Hand made T. H. Saunders
Printer: Curwen Studio
Publisher: Orde Levinson Fine Art

Mother and Child with Wave Background I (Hard Grey) 1976
Image Size 6 7/8 x 10 3/8 ins. (17,46 x 26,35 cm)
Paper Size 16x21 ins. (40,64 x 53,34 cm)
5 colour Lithograph
Edition of 40 plus 10 artist's proofs
Paper: Hand made T. H. Saunders
Printer: Curwen Studio
Publisher: Orde Levinson Fine Art

Mother and Child with Wave Background II (Yellow) 1976
Image Size 6 7/8 x 10 3/8 ins. (17,46 x 26,35 cm)
Paper Size 16x21 ins. (40,64 x 53,34 cm)
5 colour Lithograph
Edition of 40 plus 10 artist's proofs
Paper: Hand made T. H. Saunders
Printer: Curwen Studio
Publisher: Orde Levinson Fine Art

Mother and Child with Wave Background III (Soft Grey) 1976
Image Size 6 7/8 x 10 3/8 ins. (17,46 x 26,35 cm)
Paper Size 16x21 ins. (40,64 x 53,34 cm)
5 colour Lithograph
Edition of 40 plus 10 artist's proofs
Paper: Hand made T. H. Saunders
Printer: Curwen Studio
Publisher: Orde Levinson Fine Art

Reclining Figure with Stormy Sky 1975
Image Size 6¼ x 9½ ins. (15,87 x 24,13 cm)
Paper Size 15x18½ ins. (38,10 x 47,00 cm)
7 colour Lithograph
Edition of 50 plus 10 artist's proofs
Paper: Hand made T. H. Saunders
Printer: Roy Crossett
Publisher: Orde Levinson Fine Art

Introduction

This portfolio of lithographs was a happy culmination of events. It evolved spontaneously and was not dispassionately commissioned.

The uncontrived nature of the artist/dealer interaction has resulted in a rare offering that merits a special place in the history of Henry Moore.

In the graphic studio at Much Hadham, David Mitchinson showed me the lithographs that were available. There were nine, dating from 1975. I found selection difficult. When I discarded one it reappeared of its own accord, demanding further consideration. Eventually it was suggested that I reflect on them for a week.

After walking around the estate to see some new sculptures we returned to the studio. I mentioned that I always try to reach a personal understanding and appreciation of the artists with whom I am in contact, by means of discussions with them. It makes the relationship more satisfying and rewarding.

Bearing this in mind I asked if Henry Moore would care to talk about his graphic work in general and more specifically the lithographs in question. Indeed he was prepared to do so. Fortunately a tape recorder was at hand. The lithographs were then placed on the studio table and the ensuing conversation is related in the text.

It was a conversation and not an interview and the purpose of transcribing it is to convey the flow of thoughts and ideas of the artist. The reader should use it as a spring-board to the understanding of Moore's graphic work and not as an explanation of it. The lithographs speak for themselves.

The photographs, taken informally with my pocket instamatic camera, are included to add a further dimension.

I then expressed my strong conviction that all nine lithographs should be published in a portfolio counterpointed by the recorded text and photographs. It seemed to me that the lithographs, text and photographs demanded to be presented as such. Henry Moore and David Mitchinison were intrigued by the idea. We all felt that the projected portfolio had an almost Gestalt air about it – a wholeness, a necessary completeness.

We contemplated the lithographs. It was apparent that although the themes and images were diverse, the proposed portfolio was special in that it contained what was central and recurrent in Henry Moore's art: the reclining figure, the seated figure, the mother and child, and the form within a form. Moreover there were new ideas: The three lithographs where colours were indicative of mood are discussed by Moore in the text and point to their intercalary existence. Moore has here shown how apparently minor changes can have a major impact on the viewer. We all felt that each lithograph had its own individual quality and that it was important to include the three in the portfolio. Then there is, as well, the unique Woman with Dove, where the artist filled in on the same lithograph the image he normally leaves to the viewer to complete in his imagination. The portfolio provided both an illuminating flashback on Henry Moore's work as well as a fresh and new perspective. It was therefore eminently suited as a special tribute to Henry Moore on his 80th birthday. The concept was complete.

This publication was made possible by the wholehearted collaboration of Henry Moore and David Mitchinson which I was privileged to enjoy. Here I should like to express my appreciation to David Mitchinson for his enthusiasm and advice regarding the portfolio.

May I add that it was not my intention to ask Henry Moore details about his life and work – nor do I feel that all was explored regarding these graphics or will be. All I can say is that we met, conversed, and the portfolio was born.

I trust that it will mean as much to others as it does to me, reflecting not just the greatness of this artist and his classical spirit, but also his kindness, humility, warmth and patience. This encounter has enriched my life. I can only hope that the portfolio will do the same for all who see it.

I thank Henry Moore.

Orde Levinson, 1978

The Nine Lithographs

The lithographs reproduced on the following pages are not true to actual size. Full publication details are given at the beginning of this book.

Woman with Book

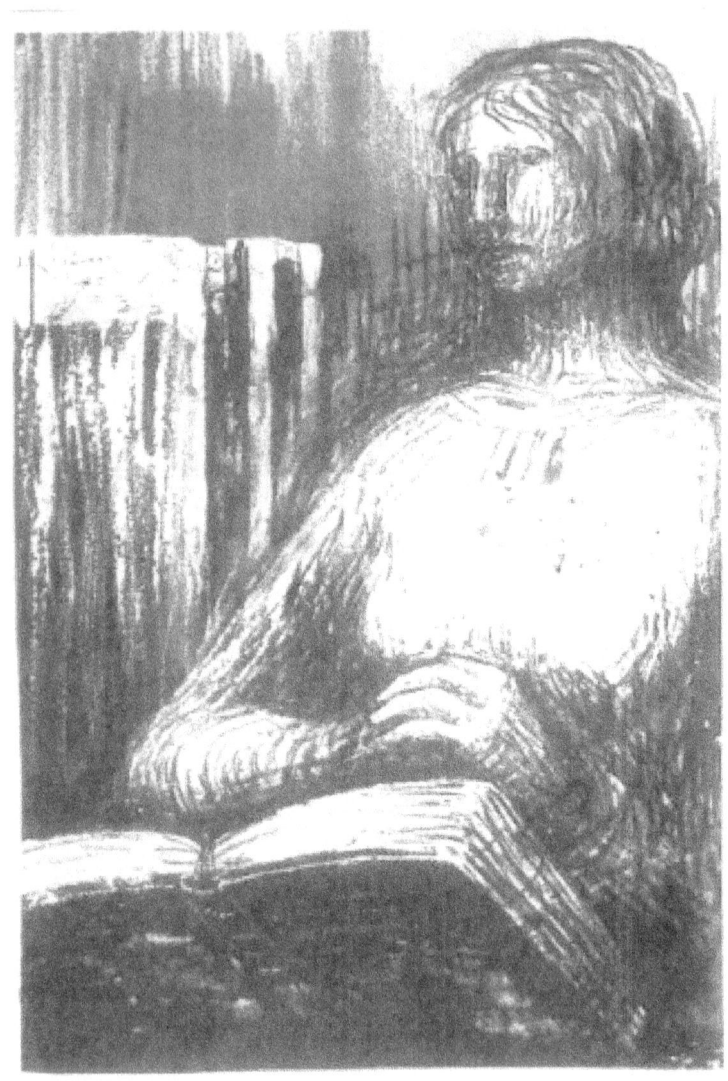

Woman with Arms Crossed

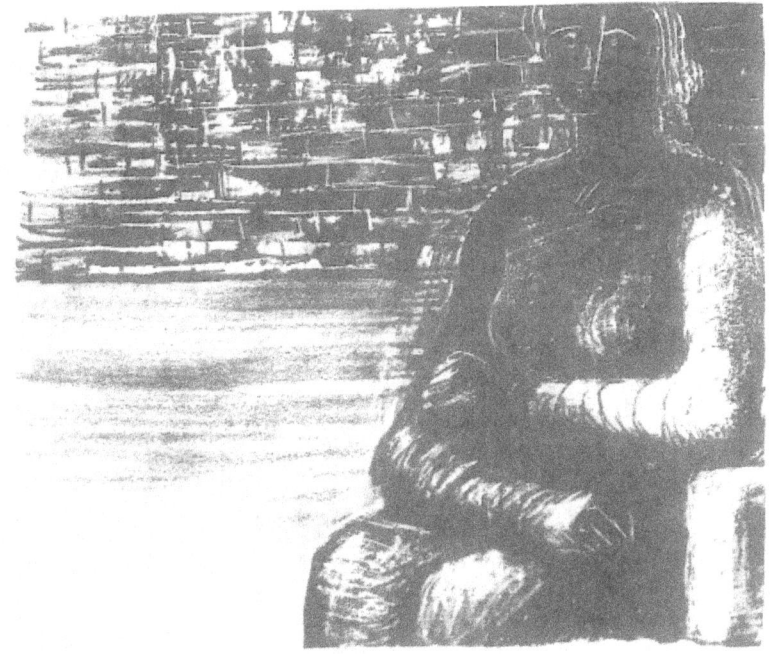

Woman with Clasped Hands

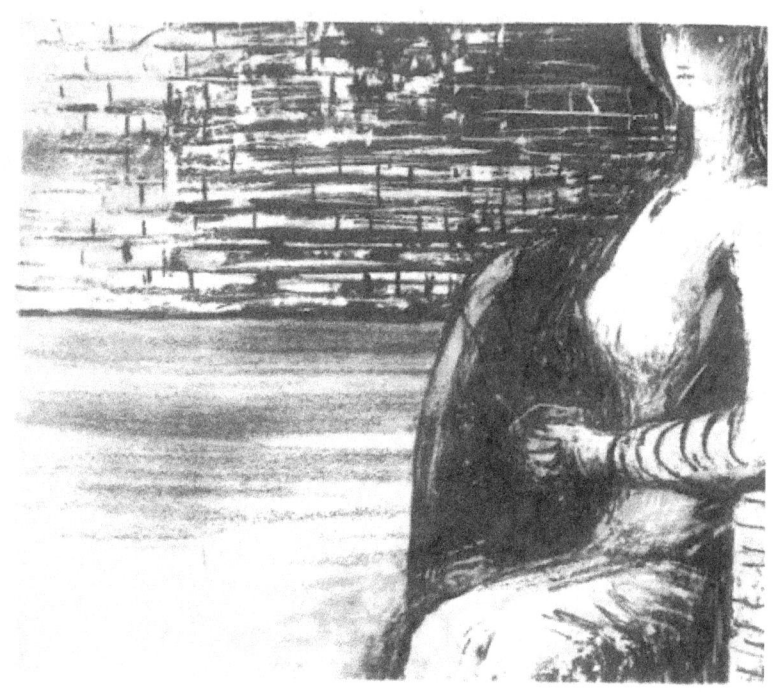

Two Seated Figures Against Pillar

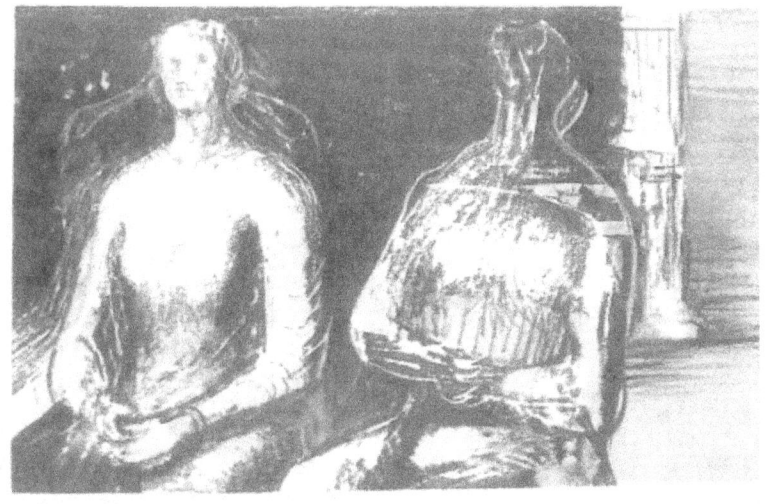

Woman with Dove

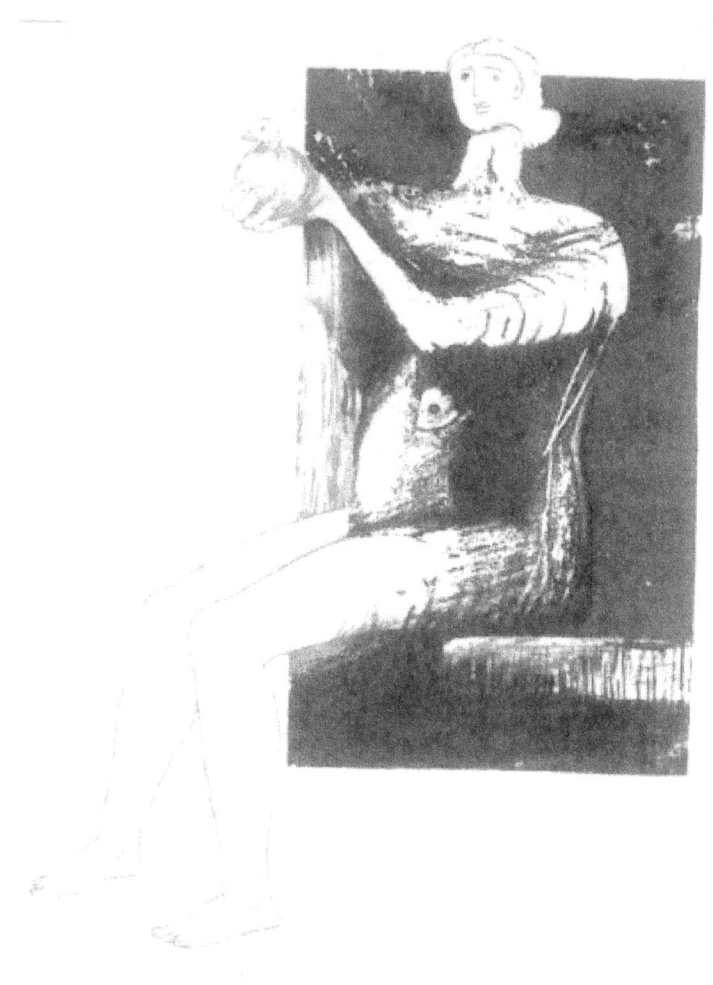

Mother and Child with Wave Background I

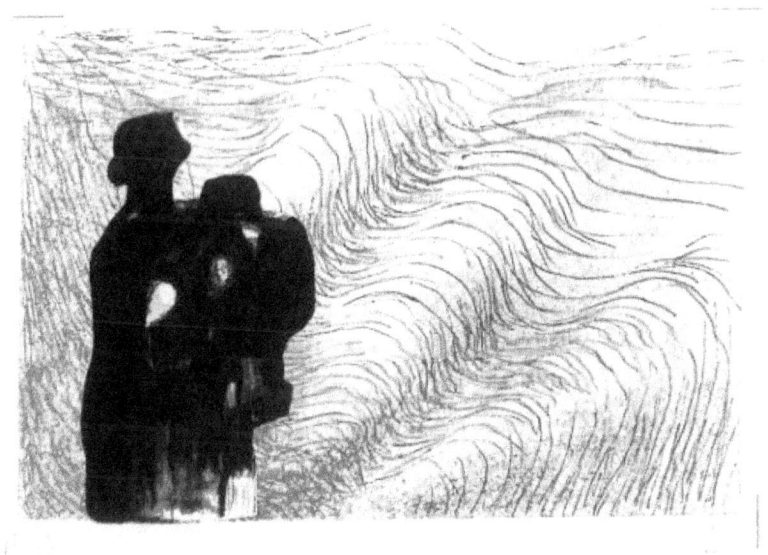

Mother and Child with Wave Background II

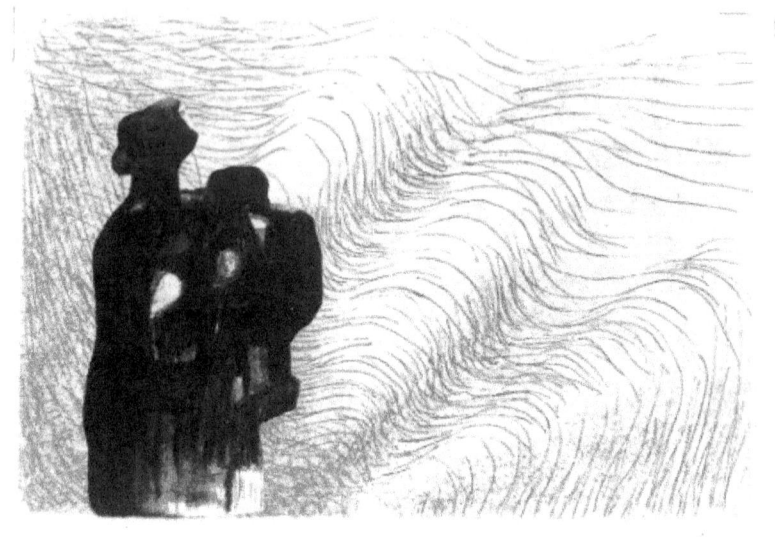

Mother and Child with Wave Background III

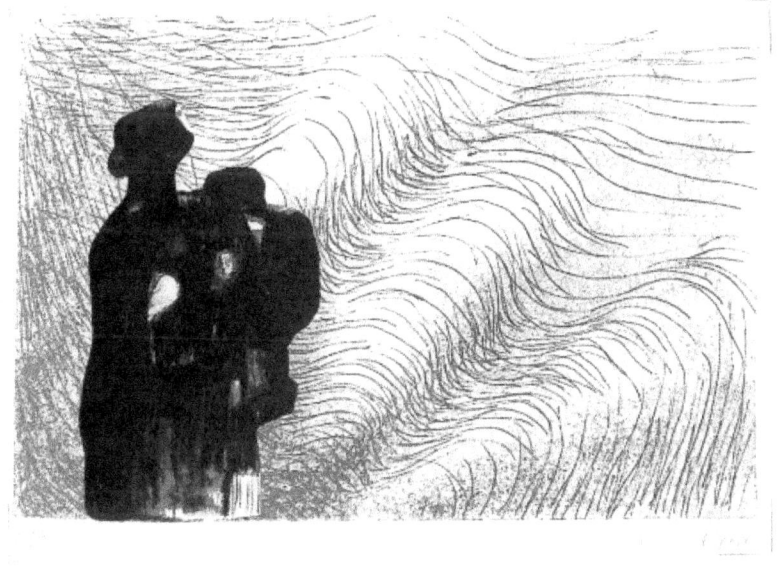

Reclining Figure with Stormy Sky

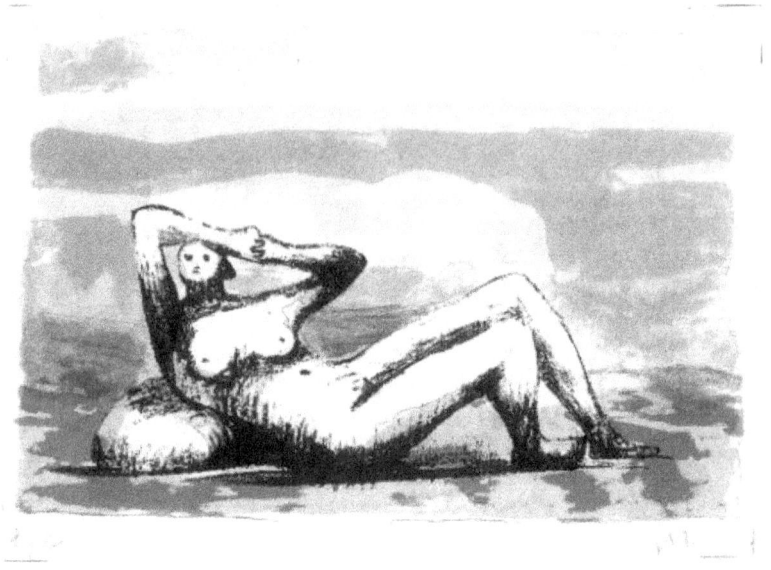

orde's Conversations with Henry Moore

Henry Moore enters the graphic studio after seeing off some of his many daily visitors.

H.M.   There now, they were nice, they were, very very humble and very grateful – one or two of them did quick sketches of me – I had to sign them.

D.M.   Oh dear. They'll go round with lots of self-portraits. (Laughter)

O.L.   I saw some of the maquettes that you were working on – they are really superb.

H.M.   Oh well, we are playing around. I enjoy the maquette stage because if one is good out of four – that's only three days lost – they take a day each. It's the big ones in which one begins to be disappointed. Then it's a long pukka three months' work. Now what... (Indicating the lithographs)

O.L.   What I would like you to consider is not a catalogue, but something informative.

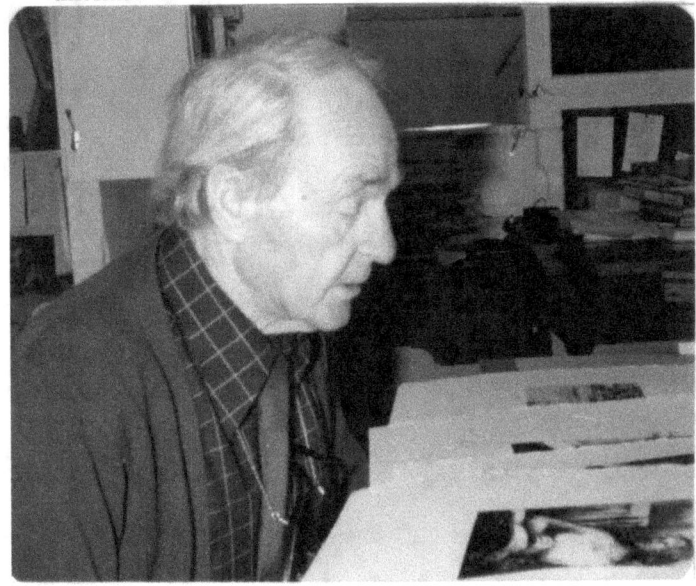

H.M.   Yes – let's begin. Often an idea can't be realised as well as you think it in your imagination, and therefore often I do a series of attempts or trials on the same idea, and this lot are all the same thing, of a figure seated in a rough kind of room – I mean a brick-walled room – but only partially in the picture, so that one gets, as it were, the corner of the room with the figure, leaving you things to imagine.

In one case I myself wanted to know what the figure was doing in that position, and so outside the frame of the picture I completed it. She seemed to be looking at something, she seemed to be expressing some kind of rather nervous tenderness in her face as I looked at it, and I completed it by imagining that she was holding a dove and that she was in the nude, and for me that was an amusing idea, but also an idea of suggesting to other people what they could do with the other ones, try to complete the picture for themselves. And the whole series is on that idea of a partial figure in a room, but enough of the room and enough of the figure to give you some sense of reality.

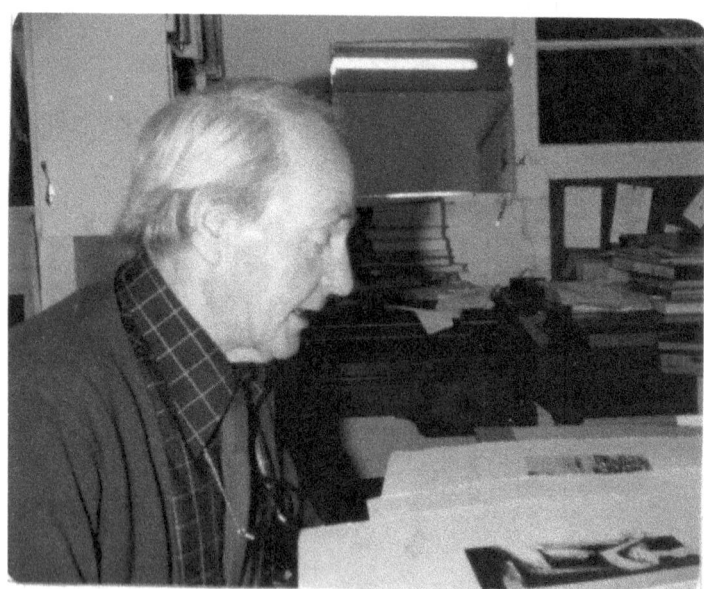

(Henry Moore studying Reclining Figure with Stormy Sky) This – I have several themes which recur in my work over and over again. That is, like all artists, I have some obsessions and the reclining figure is one of those that recur most of all; the mother and child is another of the recurring themes, another is the form inside a form, leaving the mystery of the light in it, and leaving something to the imagination. This is one of the reclining figures, and sometimes the idea is a sculptural idea. Most of my reclining figures have in my mind a sense of reality, so that I could make them into sculpture. Sometimes to make it more real still, I put the figure, the reclining figure, into a little bit of setting, into a landscape or a room or somewhere, just to give an atmosphere and give the other side – the fact that it has got another side.

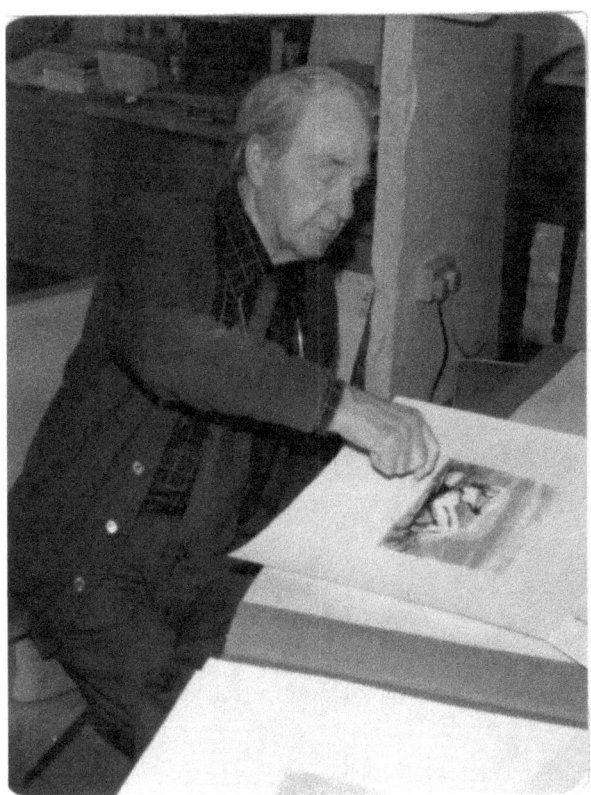

This one is the mother and child idea – being at the seaside with the waves coming in. One of the things about graphic work, particularly lithographs, is that you can very easily alter it. You see, if you change a drawing, if you make alterations in a drawing, those alterations are final, you can't go back to what it was before, except by remembering and trying to wipe it out and put it back again. But with the graphic work I can try... because I have all the plates for the different colours – the figure on a separate plate, the linear part of the waves on another plate. Here was this trial, seeing how different a thing looks if you make the waves have a yellowness, or you make them have a redness or a blackness. There's a different mood, and in this case I tried three different backgrounds, three different colours, and I shall make an edition of all three of the colours.

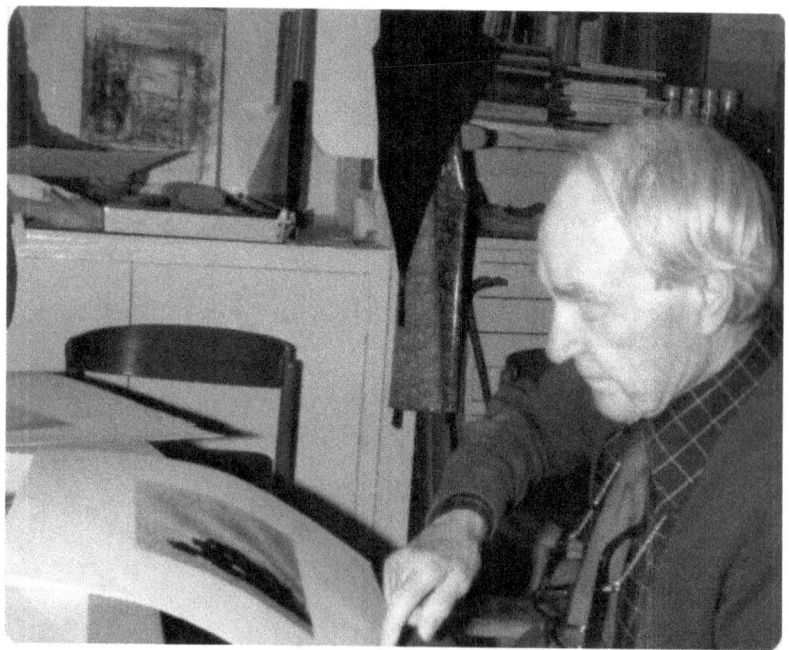

O.L.   There is no preconceived idea that you are going to do it in three different colours?

H.M.   No, no. Often a day begins and I don't know what I am going to do that day, and one may change something that one began the day before into something completely different. You can't do that, of course, with a very large sculpture, and that is why I make perhaps

twenty little maquettes, little ideas that I can hold in my hand, and therefore can do quickly, because they are on a small scale, and I can turn them over and look at them from underneath and on top and everywhere else, and consider them three-dimensionally more easily, than I can a big work. You have to get up and walk around, and lift it up and try to look and so on. I mean, it's much easier to control and to be absolute master from every point of view on a small sculpture in one's hand. This is the reason why I do maquettes before the large ones. Once you begin a very large sculpture, then you can't – like an architect — suddenly decide that you are going to put a tower at the other end of, say, a church, different to the one thought of, because he will not have made the foundations to do it. The same applies to some extent, to a very large sculpture. You can't make tremendous alterations – therefore perhaps
only one out of twenty of the maquettes that I make, well, perhaps only one out of ten is made in the next size, the one I call 'working model5, but it is only one out of twenty that arrives at the over life-size stage, and the other nineteen remain as maquettes. The working model is medium size: anything from one foot six inches to four foot. No sculptor can make a large sculpture on his own — he can't turn it – he must have assistants, just as an architect does not do all his own brick-laying, otherwise he'd never finish. So when it comes to a large sculpture, my assistants help, but they can't work from a little maquette, because any calculations they make could be so wrong if that is multiplied by twenty, whereas if I have made a medium size, then it's easy to see where things go wrong.

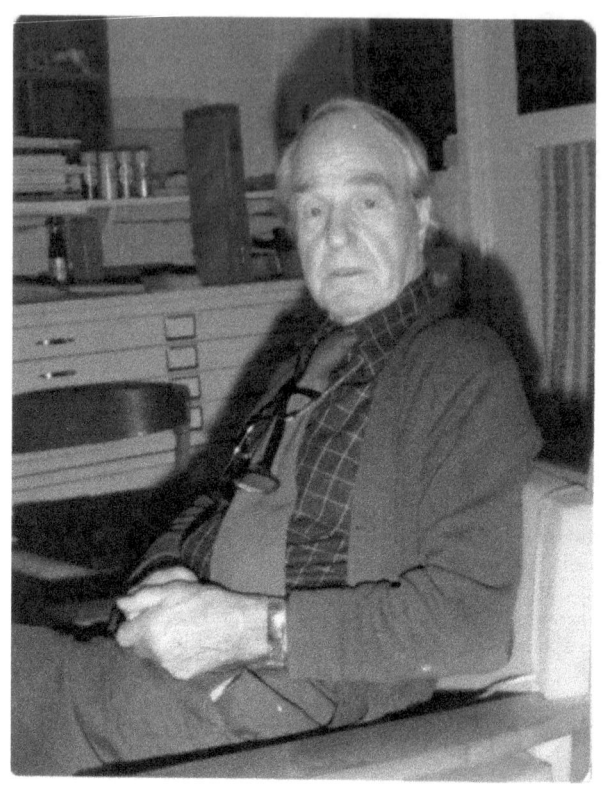

O.L.   (Referring to Woman with Dove). To go back to the one graphic where you took it a step further – as far as I know, you have not done that before?

H.M.   I might have done – If I liked this idea, this idea of the mother and child, which has a rather block-like square rhythm in it, if I liked it enough I might try to make a sculpture from it. Being a sculptor, I could turn most of my graphics into sculpture. If I decided that this was an idea, I might draw the remainder of the figure, take the top part and complete the figure.

O.L.   I meant that it was rare, because it had been actually done on the same lithograph.

D.M.   Yes, you actually see the complete image on the one lithograph. This is the only one where it has actually happened.

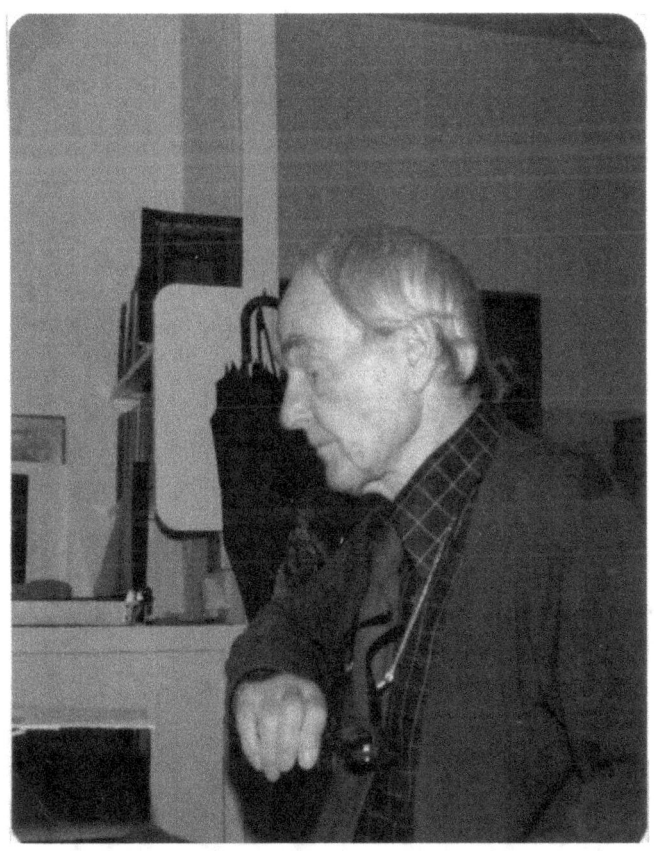

O.L.   Your graphic work: how do you view it?

H.M.   Graphic work to me is exactly the same as drawing, lithography and etching. The technical side is interesting and is special in a way. I remember as a student of the Royal College of Art, in the 1920's, graphics really meant mainly etching or lithographs, in fact, mainly etching – and I remember that the students at the College were supposed to draw every evening from 4-6 p.m. The specialist schools went on during the day and it provided the possibility for the students to leave what they were doing – sculpture and so on — and to go into the College and draw from life. It was really a very good idea. Quite a lot of the students in the sculpture school tried to get out of it, because they could pretend that they were going on with something of a specialist nature. A student of the sculpture school would say: "I want to finish this..." because a lot of them did not like drawing, because drawing made them know how bad they were, and they did not like to be reminded of this. Besides those in the sculpture school, a lot of the students in the etching school never came to the life drawing classes. In the etching school they were taught all the tricks, of making a thing look like an etching they admired. That is, they were taught the style of an etching, and if, for some reason, they admired Whistler as an etcher, or whoever it was, you could see that they were copying this artist in his way – and so they were trying to realise the etching tricks that made it look like that, and they were also being taught how to knock up a plate from the back. If you have made some mistake, you can then knock up the plate and flatten it again, and make a change there.

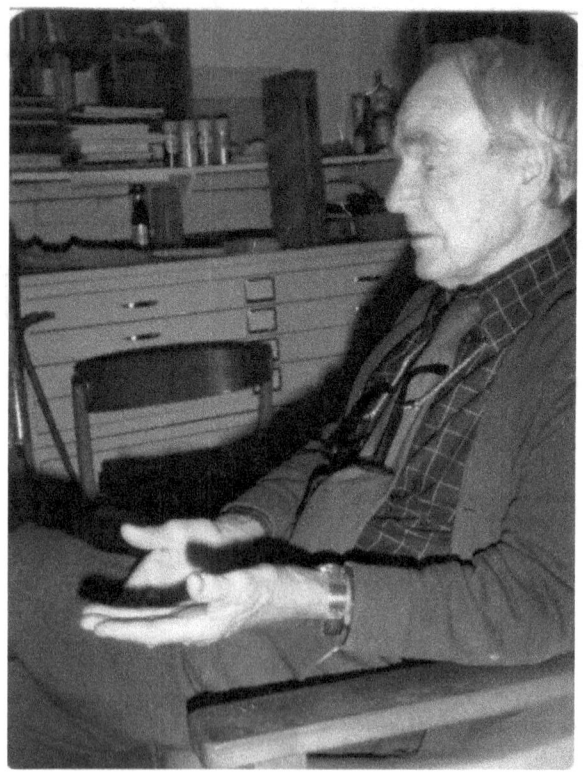

Now, all these tricks of the trade would not have been needed if they could draw – because if they could, they would not want to imitate the style of somebody else – so all I am leading up to, is that drawing is the basis of etching and lithography – of all graphic work which pretends to be more than just decoration. If you draw well, you can etch well, because it is only using a finerpoint. The technical side of all these things is simple, it is not a problem, you can enjoy them, you can enjoy exploiting them and using their special qualities even to have an inspiration. You can get new ideas that you would not get otherwise. But the real fundamental ideas are based on drawing, and drawing is based on the understanding of three-dimensional form, and that is why sculptors really should be even more concerned with drawing than painters.

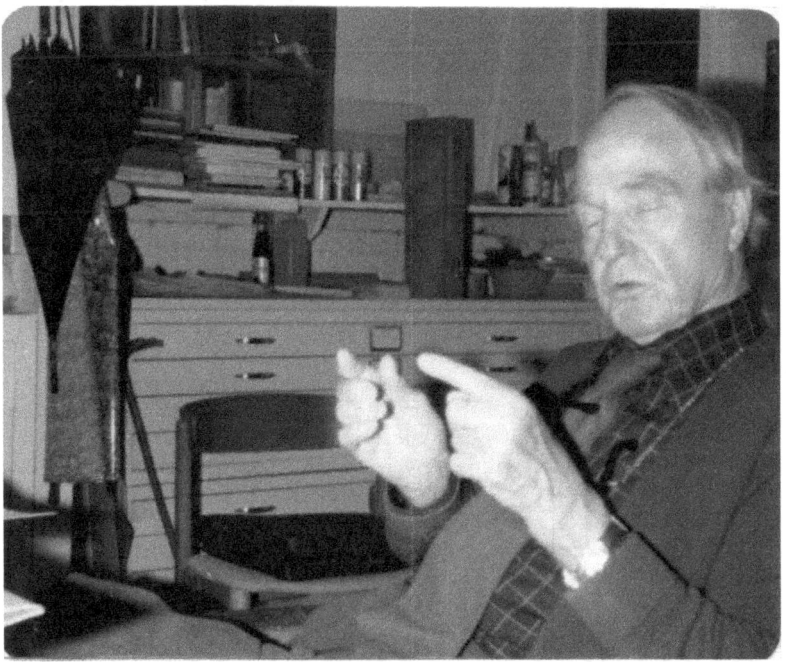

I got a letter from a painter in Finland the other day, who knew our teachers, and he said he did not like drawing, and he never did drawing. He said: "I'm interested in colour" — well, now, that is all right, a person might be interested only in colour and in the relations of colour, and perhaps he can leave drawing out of it, but somewhere he has to decide the shape of the colour and he's got to decide if he wants the colour to come forward or to go back, or whatever. I said to him the reason why I am a sculptor is that three-dimensional form is the biggest excitement and obsession for me – I mean, one can't look at anything without looking at it three-dimensionally. I am a sculptor and he is probably a painter and simply a painter, because it is colour that is important.

O.L.   I think that although colour is important in painting, the arrangement of forms in the painting is of primary importance. That is the expression of volume on a flat surface. The problem of representing a three-dimensional world on a two-dimensional canvas without tricks.

H.M.   I don't see how anybody can try to cut their lives off from what is reality – we live in a three-dimensional world, and how are you going to pretend that we live in a two-dimensional world, I don't know.

O.L.   The struggle of the artist is then to put the three-dimensionality of the world on to a two-dimensional canvas?

H.M.   Yes, some of the painters do most well – to me a painter like Rothko is tremendously three-dimensional – I mean the depth and the mystery of the thing. When I first saw his work, he came here sometimes too, when I first saw a big collection of his work together, which was at the Whitechapel – it was as if at night-time you go out from a bright room into the outside; to begin with, you see nothing with your eyes. Once you start to look longer, then some things are nearer and others further, and Rothko's painting is something like that; it's got depth, but mystery depth. So I don't think one can imagine two dimensions anyhow. Even a paper has thickness.

O.L.   That leads one into all sorts of considerations. True theatre should be really three-dimensional in a sense. That is why I believe that the great Cubists, Gris, Braque and Picasso – why they favoured the circus so much, because it is three-dimensional theatre.

H.M.   Yes, yes absolutely – the theatre can do it.

O.L.   Juan Gris – do you think that there will be a re-evaluation of his place? I think he's a great artist.

H.M.   Yes, I think he's a great artist. He's not though – he's not really the real great – he's not in the Cezanne category. He could not draw as well as, say, Degas – he had not had the experience. I don't think you get what I mean by 'greatness' unless you can go for the human body – I don't think that so-called abstract art can communicate, because it does not touch on the subject.

O.L.   Gris did very few, as far as I know, portrait paintings – I think that the main ones were of his wife Josette and a couple of drawings – those were the only human figures.

H.M.   Yes, he did, towards the end of his life, the last period of his life he was doing figures, and figures that were an attempt at being more – not more expressionistic, but human, the poses were – I can't call them 'sculptural', but they were an attempt at a nobility pose, this kind of thing. He could – if he had gone on but I think he didn't have the groundwork. I don't think that anybody can do great painting or great sculpture without a real groundwork, without drawing and studying the human figure, because we get it all from our own bodies, and if somebody tries to shortcut that, then I think their work will always have something missing – for me anyhow it does.

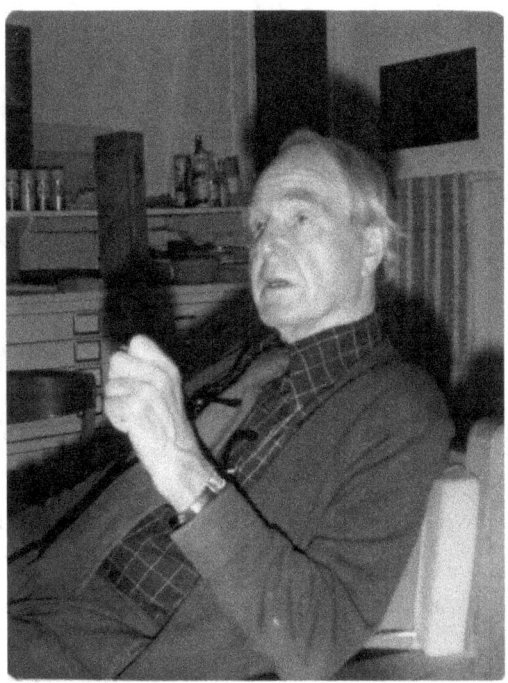

O.L.   What do you think about an artist like Jackson Pollock – I don't know if he succeeded really?

H.M.   No, but it is three-dimensional. I mean, he sees it in a three-dimensional way, the forms that were furthest away were done first – and the ones that come out on top are last – it's his way of doing it, it is a three-dimensional way. Do you get what I mean; His last drip of paint is on the top, his earlier ones fall behind. People who try to reduce the world to two-dimensions are doing – well – I don't know what – they are being theoretical and not practical.

O.L.   Your work would certainly be considered practical.

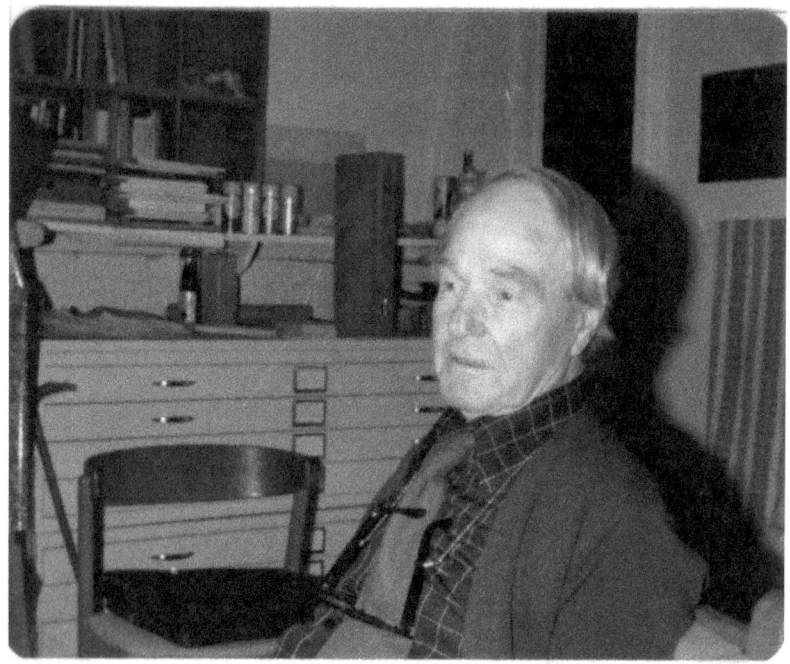

H.M.   Well, a sculptor has to be a practical person – you can't do a sculpture that falls down if you touch it – it has to stand up. You can't make a shape out of stone unless you can hold a chisel and a hammer in your hand and be a practical person. I should say that probably one of the most intellectually gifted human beings that has ever lived is Michelangelo. What he was trying to do at the end of his life in building the dome of St. Peter's-was a job in his day, as difficult as going to the moon is in our day. He was not an impractical man. I mean this idea that artists are people who dream is rubbish – it's rubbish!

O.L.   The practicality of a graphic – how do you see it?

H.M.   Well, with a graphic one has to handle a material. In lithography it can be a stone, it can be a plastic, it can be chalk or whatever else – transfer paper and so on. I mean, the processes make it a practical thing, more so even than drawing, because in a drawing you can draw on any surface. It does not matter what. The ancients drew on rocks or anything. But with a graphic, you have to have a practical attitude to it – to get it true. So a graphic work is more practical in technique than in drawing.

O.L.   A more personal question, which I hope you will not mind my asking you – most great artists, either intentionally or unintentionally, have had a predilection towards certain philosophers – they have liked reading certain philosophers or certain writers. Are there any such that you particularly admire?

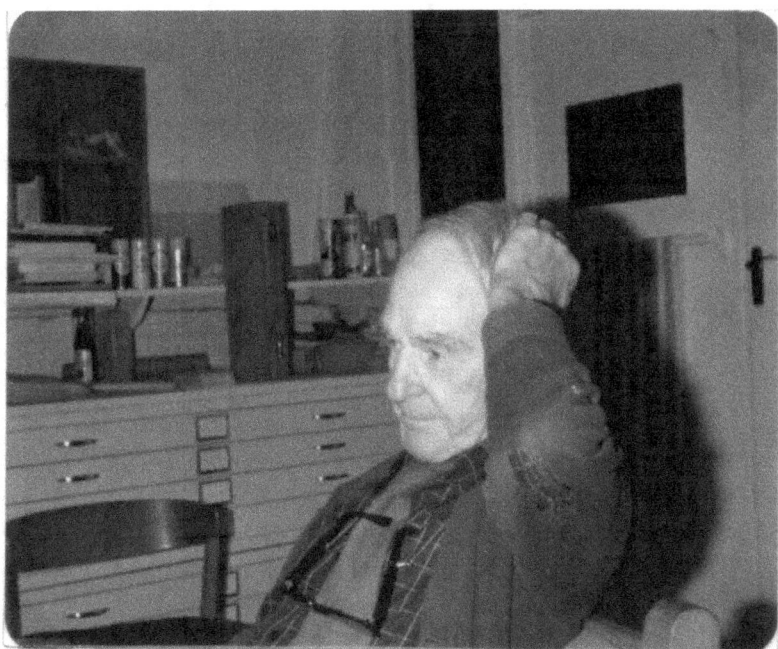

H.M.   Well, to begin with, as a young person, novelists had the biggest influence. Probably they have had the biggest influence on my life, because I think the influence you have when you are young and when you are an adolescent, is probably the most indelible of all – and the novelists I absorbed — I lived in their worlds. I lived in them one by one as a schoolboy around the age of thirteen or fourteen — it was Scott, Sir Walter Scott, more than Dickens – it was never Dickens for me. I mean, I read David Copperfield and so on, but it was Walter Scott the kind of romantic world that he made. After Scott – well – I read some of the ordinary popular schoolboy ones like Treasure Island, and so on, but those were not as real and did not mean as much to me as the Scott ones – after that the Russian novels — Dostoievsky and Tolstoy. I lived in that world, particularly Dostoievsky. I lived in that world for as long as the novel lasted, then I began the next, so that my life was coloured in this.

Then after the Russians came Thomas Hardy. I read every single novel of Thomas Hardy. After Thomas Hardy came some of the French novelists, like Stendhal. Not so much Flaubert, though I read his works. Then D. H. Lawrence – I lived in his world for a period, and all those have coloured my life even more than painting and sculpture have done. They may have had a more direct influence – but the other forms you as a human being. This is what I think is the great value of novels: it is not entertainment – the novel is not, as some people think, only there to amuse you temporarily for two or three days. The great novelists have a great influence in colouring and forming a young person for the rest of his life. So that even though Shakespeare means a lot, I think he was a later influence for me. Seeing the plays of Shakespeare came later than the novelists. The Shakespeare that you do at school is too much a subject.

Later, I never read any novels. Only those given to me by friends I read out of duty. Otherwise certain books, like this one I have just re-read, and have read at least four times in my life – is Eckerman's "Conversations with Goethe". I have never read much Goethe – I have not read Faust all the way through, but then ten years ago I read Eckerman's "Conversations with Goethe", which gives Goethe's attitude to life – and it's a marvellous book – a wonderful book. I read it again and again because it is so wise – it's so full of digestive experience that he's thought over and over, and for me that is the kind of book and that is the kind of influence that is most important.

O.L.   You mentioned how important the writer is – there I agree with you, and I think too, that art has a function. You can't expect to be pleased by art – the viewer, I feel, has just as much duty as the painter...

H.M.   Yes.

O.L.   To understand, to look at, and appreciate.

H.M.   Yes.

O.L.   There is a very strong interlink between painting and poetry and music. The true painter, the true poet – all have a sort of similar sense of life for want of a better word.

H.M.   Yes, well I think painting, sculpture, poetry and music – all the arts – dancing – all the arts, they are to make human beings appreciate the human side of life other than the practical making a living. I mean, other than getting food. Every animal has to work – it eats all day long, that's work. No, I think that painting and sculpture are there to make us use our eyes and find, by using our eyes, the world to be a wonderful place, and to have unknown things to discover and to try to understand them. And music is to make us use our ears other than getting out of the way when a motor-car hoots and so on. In fact, the arts are there to make life – to make human beings think about life, experience life, get more out of it than animals can do.

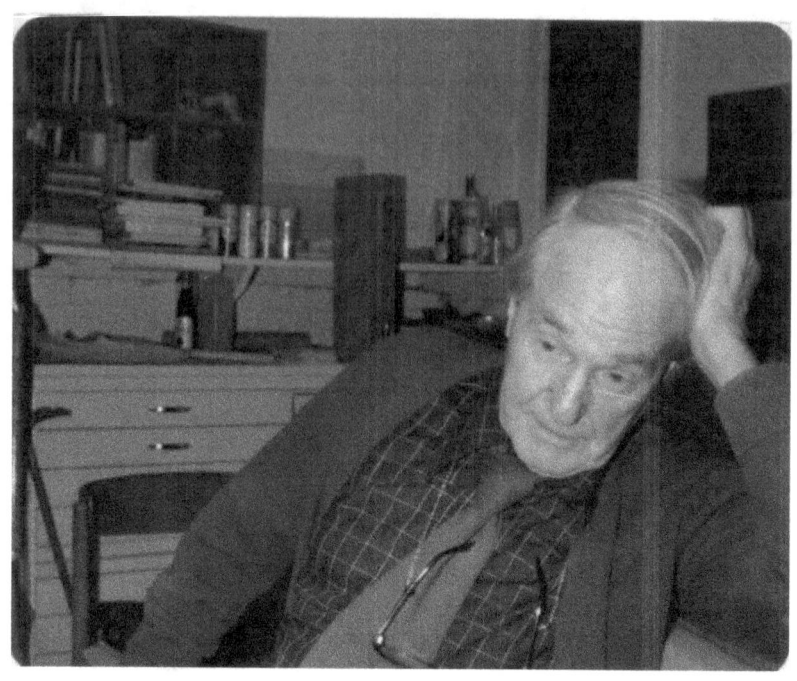

O.L.   Would you go a step further, perhaps, and say almost that art
        creates the world?

H.M.   Yes – we all know this: if a child by accident loses its parents, and
        there have been one or two instances of children being brought up
        by animals – all they do is grunt and crawl and behave exactly like
        an animal. Human beings learn it all from the past even the lowest
        of human beings. Language – everything – is the sum total of the art
        of human beings doing things other than just getting food. It's this,
        the whole of human experience, and you pick it up – you pick it up
        very quickly.

        There are some young artists who think that they don't need the
        past. I remember a contemporary of mine – we were walking past
        the National Gallery one day, and he said: "Henry, there's our
        enemy" – meaning that we were fighting the "old masters", meaning
        we were trying to do without them. One of my assistants told me of
        a student who said: "My object is to kick old Henry Moore in the
        teeth." You see, sometimes people think that they can do without
        the past, and then they get this attitude that the past is their enemy,

knowing that the past is what they got everything from. And I say that if they were brought up by an animal, and did not have all the illimitable experiences that the world has brought into language, brought into painting, all this they take in without knowing, so that for anyone to think they can do without the past is stupid.

O.L.   The way in which one delineates who is a great artist and who is not, in terms of art history is to take a broad spectrum view and to see the influence of that particular artist on the course and development of art.

H.M.   Yes, and you'll find that the ones in my opinion who have contributed most have also owed most to the past: someone like our biggest artist, Turner. If any English artist learnt and copied from others to begin with – Turner did; really, he pillaged and stole, but it was not stealing – he was learning: and if you look at Cezanne, whom I think is the greatest contributor to art generally over the last hundred years – my goodness, one knows how much he looked. In the period of the Impressionists he was never a real, full, completely out-and-out Impressionist, say like Monet was. He said he wanted to make Impressionism an art of the museums. Now, what he meant was that when he went to the museums, Impressionism left something out – a whole lot of things that he found in the museum. We know that he looked at Rembrandt; We know that he looked at Delacroix, he looked at everybody, he looked at Nature, it's a mixture of the two – it's a mixture of living in nature and also appreciating and learning from the past.

O.L.   Would you say, too, that one also is living in one's particular period in nature: Cezanne in the 19th Century, you in the 20th Century; and you see nature differently in each particular period?

H.M.   You can't help but live in your period. Everybody lives in their own period. Blake tried to live not in his own period, but when you look at him, his paintings are like the glass paintings of his own day – it's got all the qualities of that period. We all have it. My work will be easily recognisable in 100 years' time, as of this time. Nobody can get away from his period. So you don't need to worry about staying in your period. It's like people saying "I want to be English".

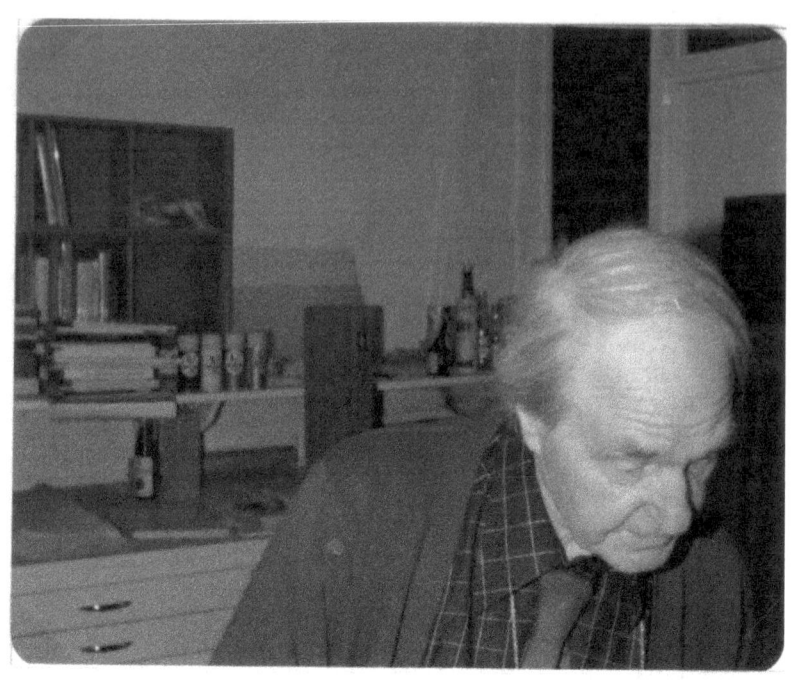

English is made up of hundreds of other things. England is changing all the time; England is changing by its connections with Europe. For someone to say "I want to stay in my own little niche", he is still in a niche. These restrictions are not valid. (Pause) Why do I think that Rembrandt, Michelangelo, Leonardo, Masaccio, Titian and so on are the great artists – and not some other ones? Is it because I think that their sense of colour is more special than anybody else's? Not at all, none of them. Is it that one thinks that they design better, or that their compositions are better, that their sense of abstraction, of organisation is better, and so on ? No, of course not. In trying to sort out what it is in their painting that is really great – I think it is their human understanding, their understanding of human nature. I mean Rembrandt – every single person that he paints or draws has a... (Henry Moore jumps up and moves to his desk and takes down a postcard: Rembrandt's "Saskia Asleep in Bed" – Ashmolean Museum, Oxford) - It's remarkable — a little sketch like this. The way the face, the hand – that hand has got sleep in it. It's the humanity of those people. The same with a novelist. It's not their cleverness in writing, it's not their cleverness in inventing plots, it's not all those things – it's their understanding of their real feeling for human beings.

O.L.   Conveying of great emotions?

H.M.   Well –

(Pause)

– Other than emotions – No – you can try to convey sorrow - No, it's the relationship of people to people – it's this belief that human life is important, that human beings are important. It's being what one would call a fundamentally religious person. That is really what all those people are – they are fundamentally religious, in the sense that they believe that life is important, and that life is worth living. They are not doing these things out of cleverness or whatever it is.

H.M.   All right; I'm going to do some work.

(He is half outside when Mrs. Moore calls inaudibly.)

H.M.   It's only half past five – I'm going back in there.

(He walks into the adjoining maquette studio.)

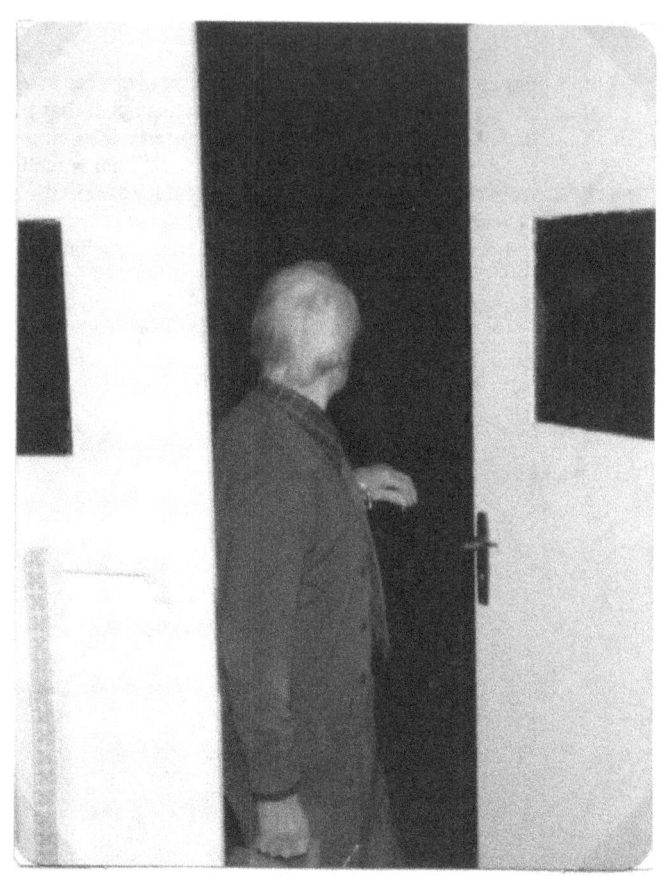

Photographs of Henry Moore at Much Hadham

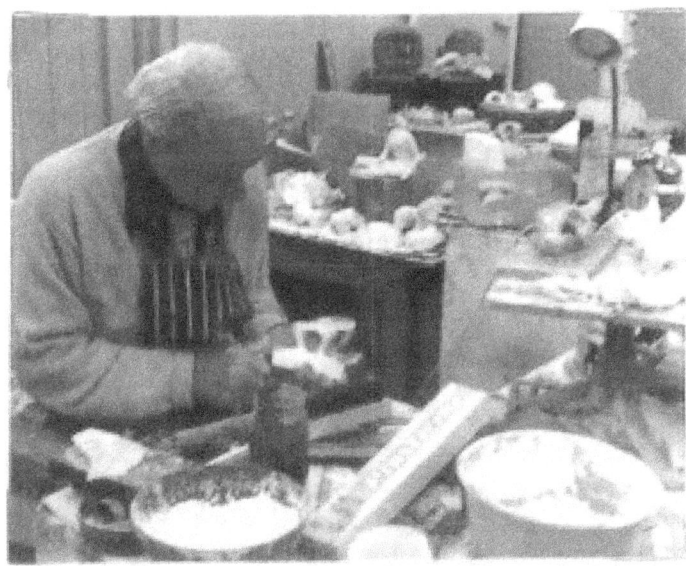

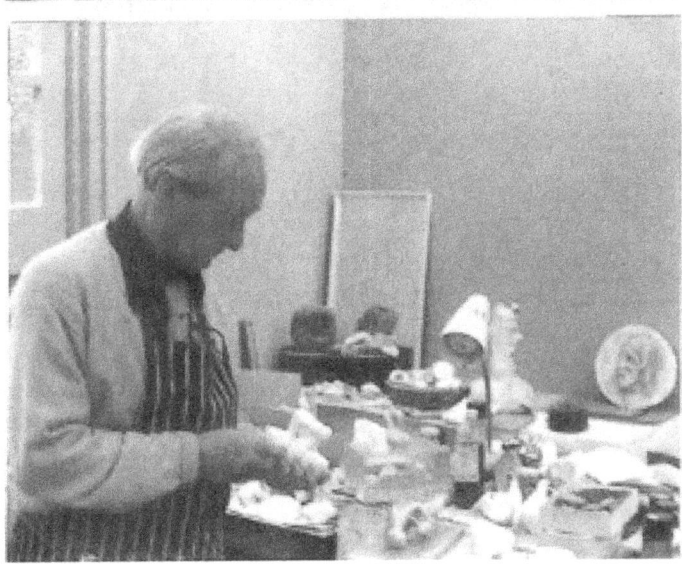

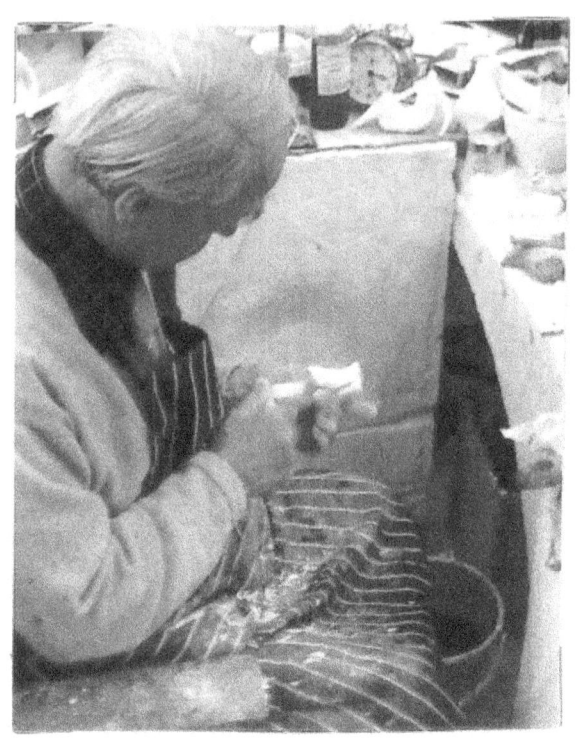

44

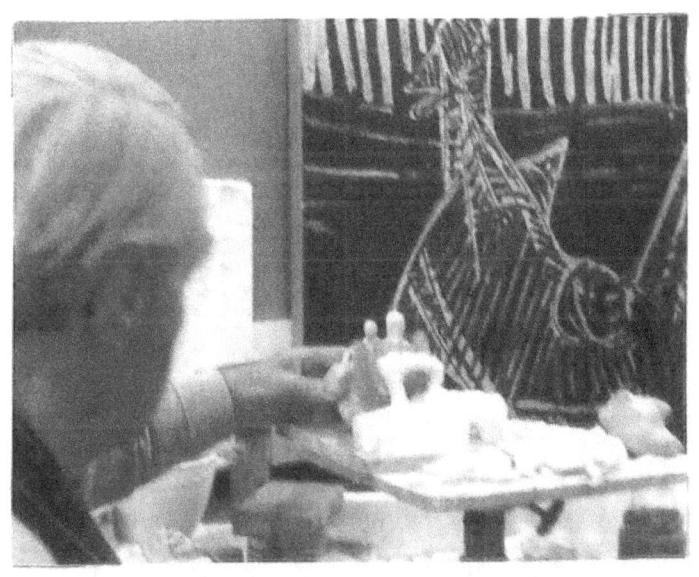

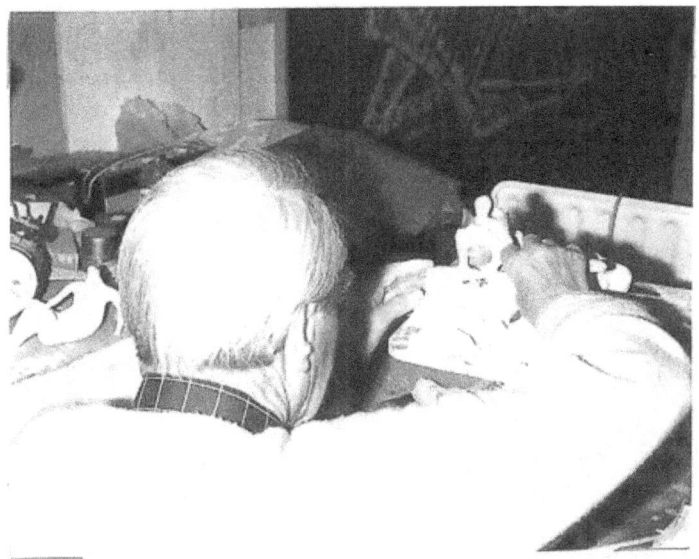

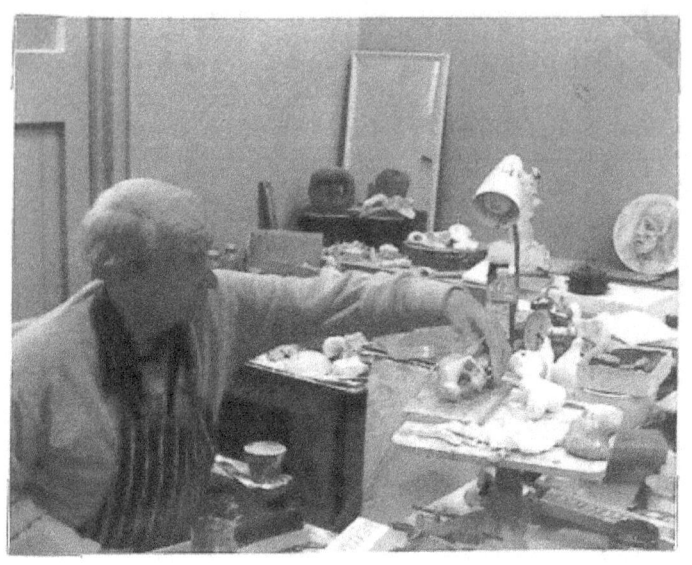

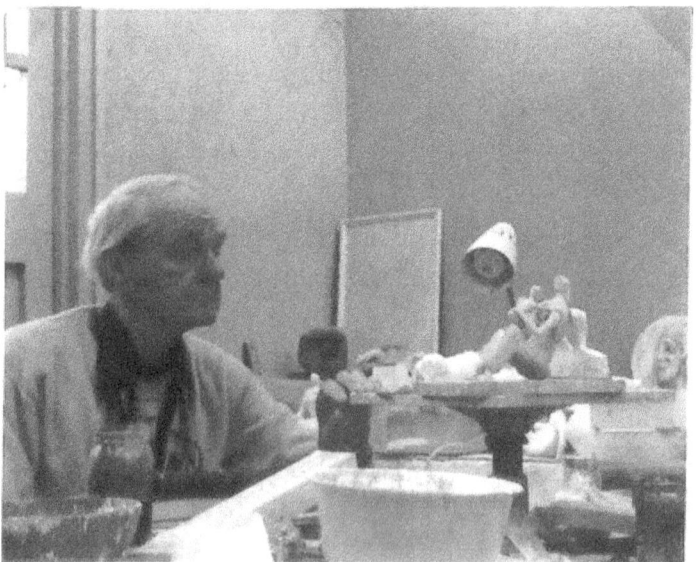

Paperback Edition

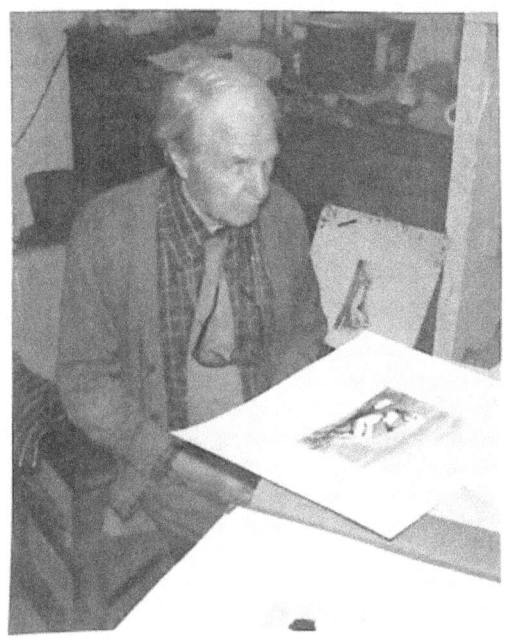

Introduction

The themes and images of this portfolio may at first glance appear diverse. However, the selection has a completeness which matches the retrospective spirit of an 80th birthday publication.

The central themes of the mother and child, seated and reclining figures and forms within forms recur throughout the art of Henry Moore. In the 'Mother and Child with Wave Background' I, II and III Henry Moore shows for the first time in his graphic art how a different mood is created by colour variations. 'Woman with Dove' is also a unique departure whereby on the same lithograph the artist has filled in the image normally left to the viewer's imagination.

The nine lithographs are presented with the added dimension of quotations by Henry Moore and informally taken photographs.

I thank David Mitchinson for his generous assistance and enthusiasm.

To Henry Moore, my heartfelt gratitude for his free spirit and friend-ship and for making this all possible.

Orde Levinson, 1978

orde's Conversations with Henry Moore
(Edited)

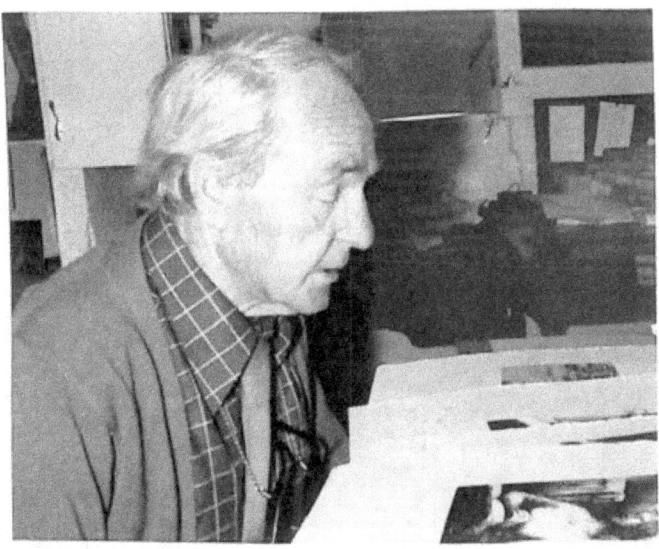

Woman with Book, Woman with Arms Crossed, Woman with
Clasped Hands, Two Seated Figures Against Pillar and Woman
with Dove

'At first attempt an idea can't always be realised as well as one
imagines it. Therefore, sometimes one does a series of trials on the
same idea. These are all on that idea of a woman seated in a rough,
brickwalled room. The partial position of the figure leaves one scope
for imagination yet there is always enough of the room and of the
figure to convey a sense of reality.'

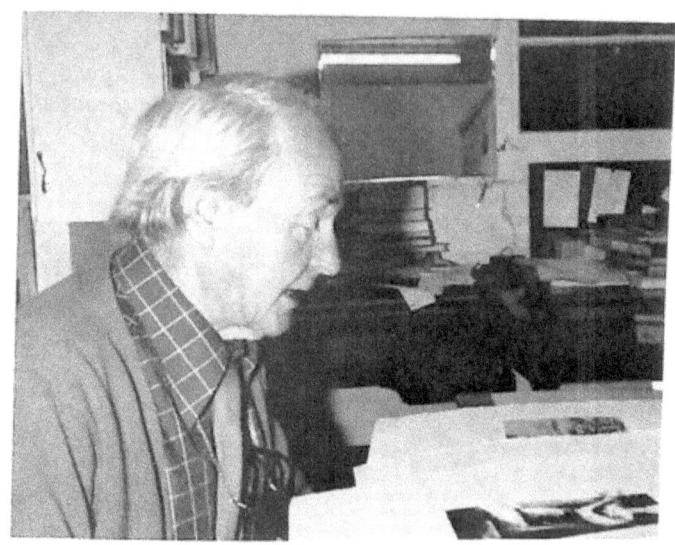

Woman with Dove

'In one case I wanted to know what the figure was doing in that position. I imagined that she was looking at something and expressing a rather nervous tenderness and so I let her hold a dove and completed the rest of the figure. This completion could be done to any of the series.'

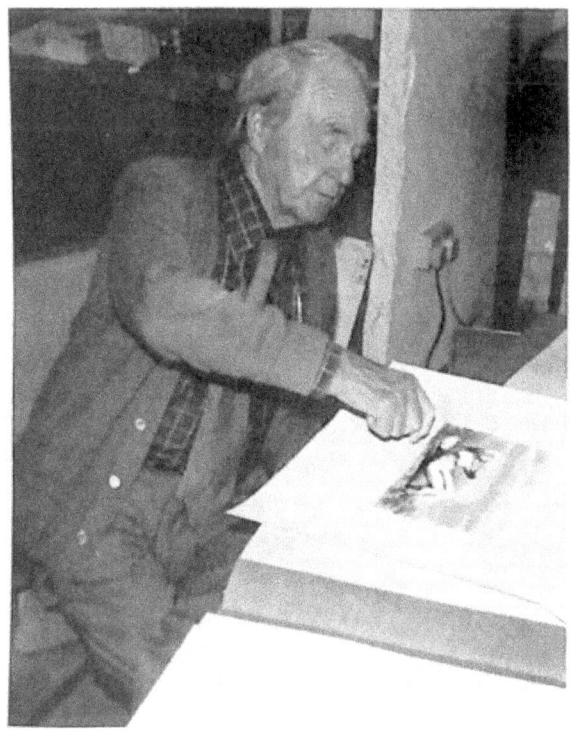

Reclining Figure with Stormy Sky

'Sometimes to make the drawing of a figure more real I put it into a setting – a three-dimensional space, a landscape or a room etc.'

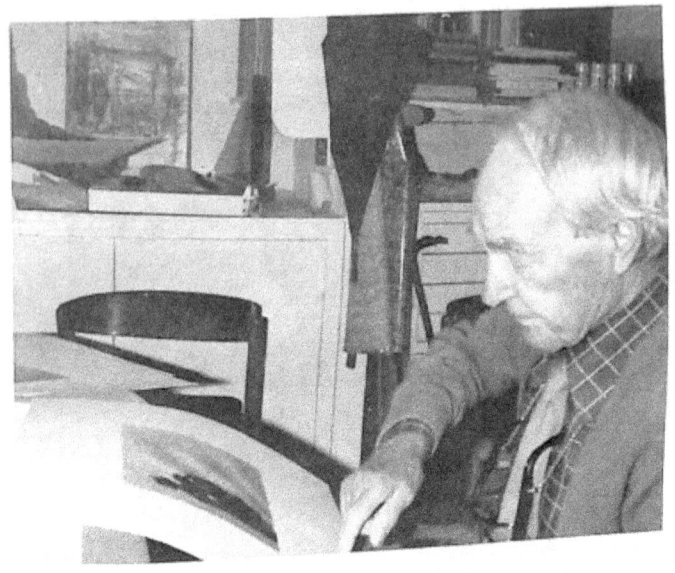

Mother and Child with Wave Background I, II and III

'This is the mother and child idea – at the seaside with the waves coming in. In an actual drawing alterations are final – you can only try to go back to what it was before by remembering and rubbing it out — whereas an advantage in lithography is that colours can be easily changed because there is a separate plate for each. Here was this trial showing how different a work looks if you change the colour – there's a different mood in each case.'

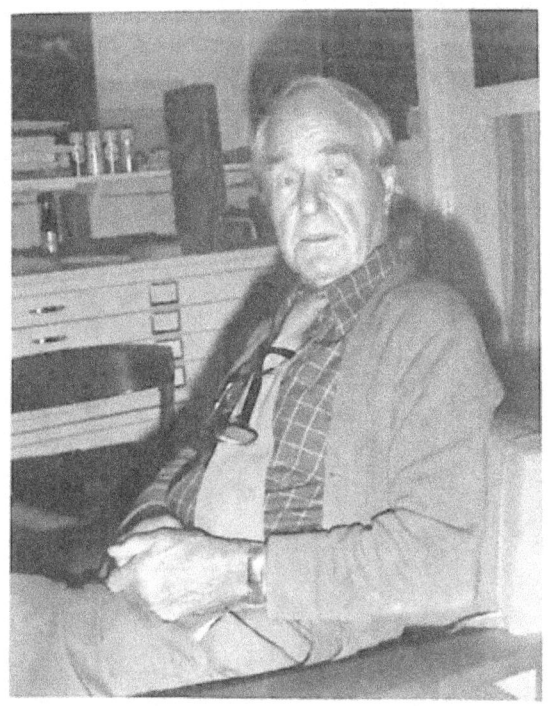

'Graphic work to me is exactly the same as drawing. If you can draw well you can etch well because it is only using a finer point. The technical side is relatively simple. The fundamental ideas are based on drawing and good drawing for me is the ability to represent three-dimensional form in space, on a flat surface – perhaps that is why I think that sculptors should be even more concerned with being able to draw than painters.'

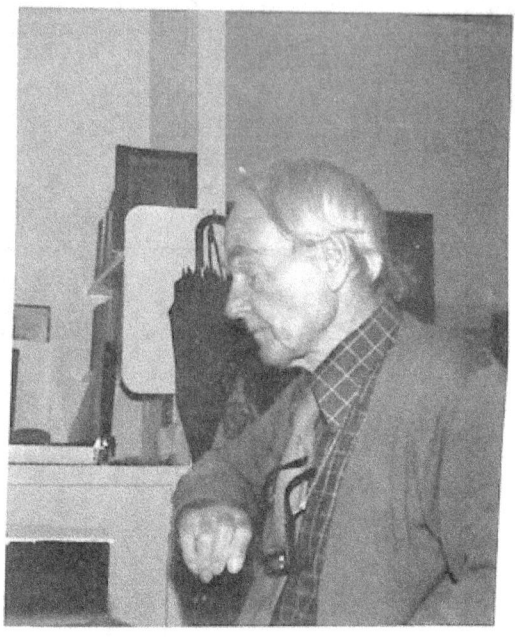

'There are several themes which recur over and over in my work. Like all artists I have some obsessions and the reclining figure is one, the mother and child is another favourite and another is the exterior-interior form – an inside form being protected by an outer form sometimes producing a mystery like a figure in a cave.'

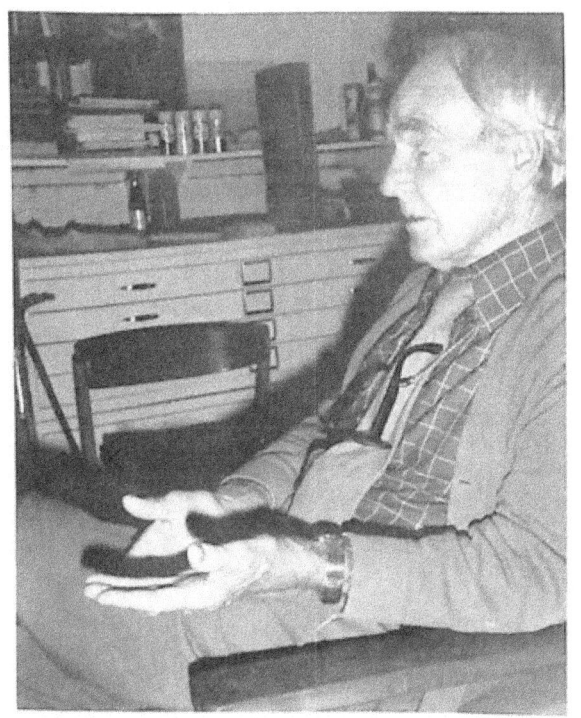

'Being a sculptor I could turn most of my graphics into sculpture
For example, this mother and child with its block-like rhythm is a
sculptural idea.'

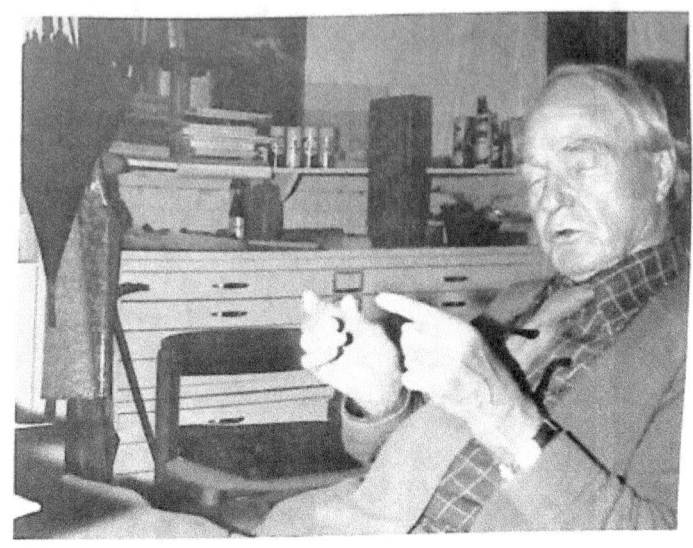

'I don't see how it is possible to cut oneself off from reality. We live in a three-dimensional world of form and space.'

'Good art is not produced in a hit-or-miss way or just by luck. It often needs great perseverance and effort, both intellectual and physical.'

'A sculptor has to be a practical person. You can't do a sculpture that falls down if you touch it. You can't make a shape out of stone unless you can efficiently use a hammer and chisel. The practical problem Michelangelo had designing and working out the Dome of St. Peters was perhaps as difficult in his day as getting a man to the moon in ours.'

'Why do I think that Giotto, Masaccio, Piero della Francesca, Leonardo, Michelangelo, Titian, Rembrandt and a few other painters and sculptors are all truly great artists? It is not any one technical attribute in their work. For me it is a bigness of spirit – a fundamental humanity, almost a religious belief expressing that life is important and wonderful and worth living.'

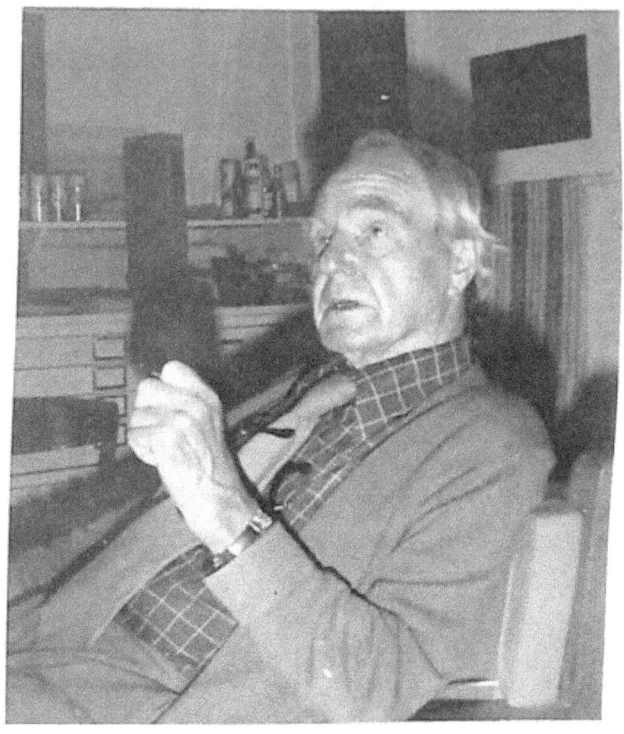

'My work is based on a knowledge and love of the human figure.
For me we get all our understanding of form from our own bodies.
If someone tries to shortcut that then, I think, their work will always
have something missing.'

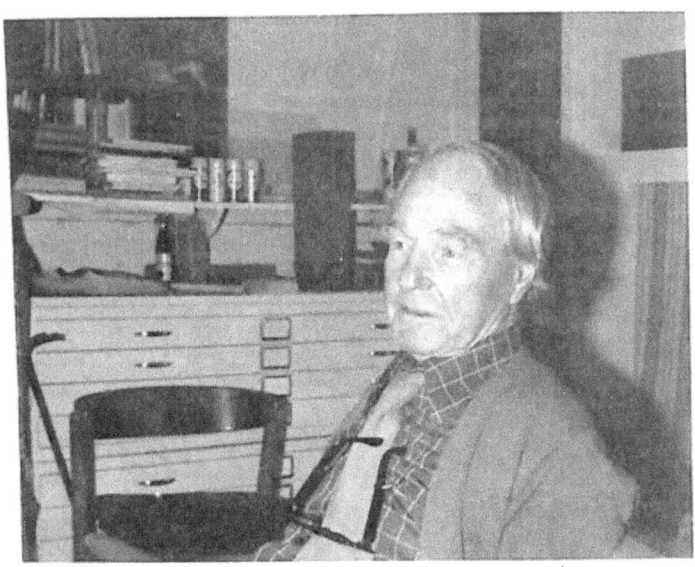

'As a young person, novels had a great influence on my life. I lived in the world of the novel for as long as it lasted, then I began the next and so my life up to the age of 20/21 was coloured in this way even more than by painting and sculpture.

As a schoolboy I lived in the romantic world of Sir Walter Scott – it was never Dickens for me. Later came the Russian novelists, Tolstoy and Dostoievsky. After them Thomas Hardy, then some of the French novelists, like Stendhal and Flaubert. Then D. H. Lawrence and so on. Today I hardly ever read novels. Certain books, however, like Ecker-man's "Conversations with Goethe" I read and re-read. It is a marvellous, wonderful book – it is so wise, so full of digested experience.'

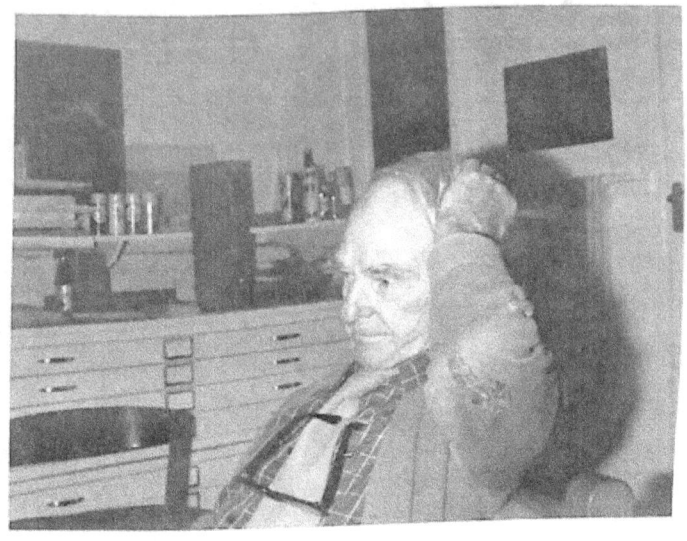

'In my opinion the artists that have been most original and have contributed most have also owed most to the past.'

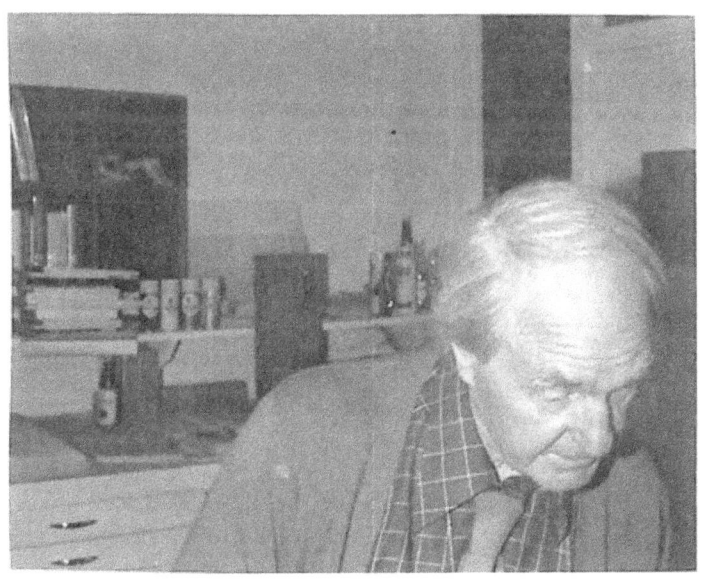

'Often a day begins and I don't know what I am going to work on that day.'

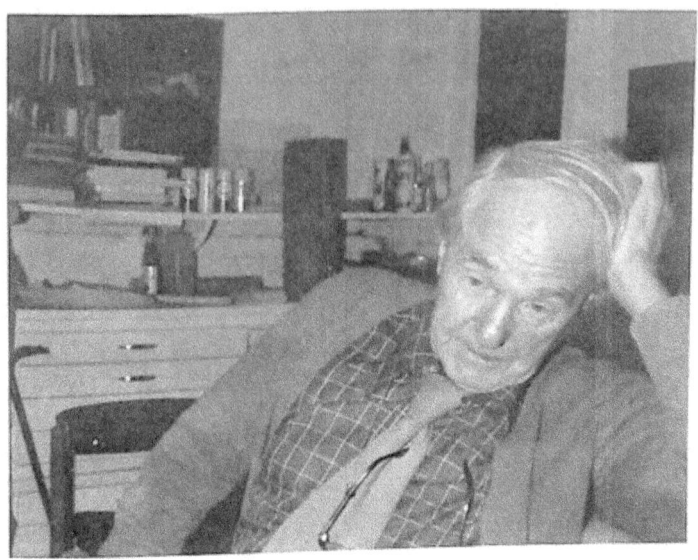

'One can't live outside one's own period. Perhaps someone like William Blake thought he could, but seeing his work now it has a strong flavour of early English nineteenth century.

'I think sculpture, painting, literature, music, drama – all the arts help to make people enjoy the wonderful side of life quite apart from the practical business of making a living and surviving – I mean, other than getting food, every animal has to work, it eats all day long, that's work.

Through our senses we can appreciate the world as a marvellous place with unknown aspects to discover. For example, music helps us to use our cars, other than simply getting out of the way when a motor car hoots. The arts help to make people think, experience and consciously appreciate the wonders of life, to get more out of our existence, one hopes, than animals do.'

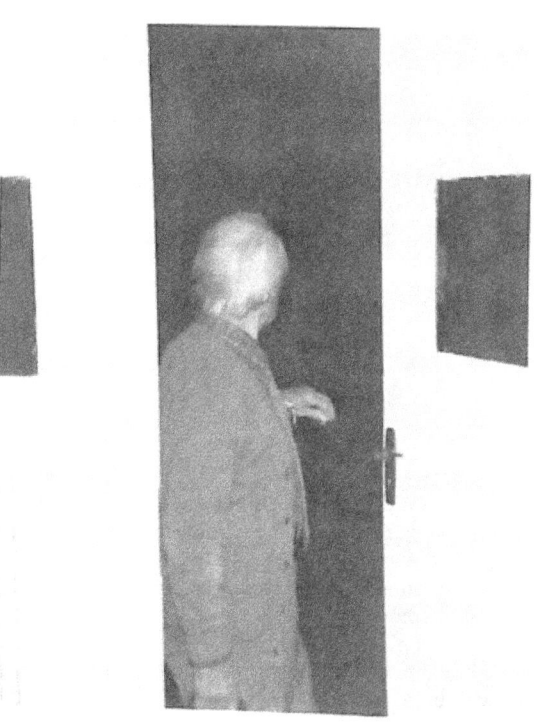

Note by the Publisher 2013

Mæg ic be me sylfum	I can make a true song
soðgied wrecan,	about me myself,

The Seafarer, date unknown.(Approximate translation of the old English)

Song, established in 2013 is an imprint of a new publication house, a division of Song of the Wild Swan Ltd.

It publishes any writings from anyone who has a song.

Song also participates in the BEL (Barter Exchange Levy) Price System.

List of Selected Works by orde

Song, November 2013
Areas of classification may overlap

Books

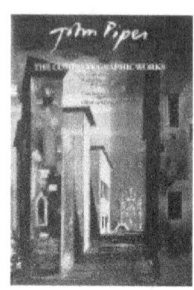

1   *John Piper – The Complete Graphic Works: A Catalogue Raisonné 1923-1983*. Compiled and edited by Orde Levinson. Faber & Faber, 1988.

2   *I Was Lonelyness: The Complete Graphic Works of John Muafangejo 1968-1987*. Struik Winchester, 1992. Foreword by Archbishop Desmond Tutu. Contributing essays from: Olga Levinson (The Life and Art of John Muafangejo); Edward Lucie-Smith (John Muafangejo); Pat Gilmour (On Not Being a Political Artist); Orde Levinson (John Muafangejo, Cubism and Traditional African

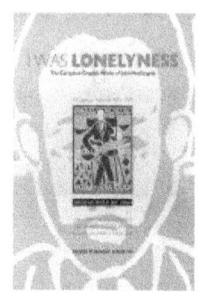

Art); Olga Levinson (The Historical Development of Art in Namibia) and Steven Sack (The Rorke's Drift Art and Craft Centre) and all Muafangejo's Interviews, Statements and published conversations.

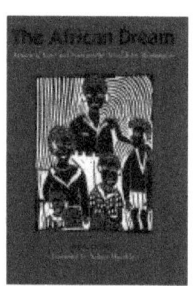

3   *The African Dream – Visions of Love and Sorrow. The Art Of John Muafangejo*. Thames and Hudson, 1993. Foreword by Nelson Mandela.

4   *Quality and Experiment. The Prints of John Piper – A Catalogue Raisonné.* Lund Humphries, 1996.

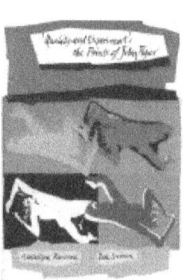

5   *The Prints of John Piper – A Catalogue Raisonné 1921-1991*. Lund Humphries, 2010. Contributing essays: Introduction (Orde Levinson); Experiment and Quality (Orde Levinson); Subject and Technique in Piper's Printmaking (David Fraser Jenkins); Working with Printers (John Piper).

6   *Hitting the Nail on the Head – The Complete Written Works of John Piper 1913-1992.* An estimated three volumes with contributing essays by various authors (tba). Scheduled for publication 2014/5.

7   *Delights and Aphorisms, selected writings of John Piper.* Scheduled for publication 2014-5.

8   *Daniel Henry Kahnweiler: A bibliography.* Scheduled for publication 2014.

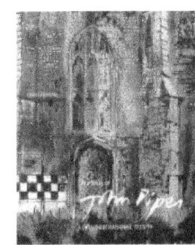

9   *The Life and Work of Daniel Henry Kahnweiler: A critical evaluation.* Originally part of the D. Phil. Study at Magdalen College, Oxford University. Scheduled for publication 2015.

10   *The Complete Writings of Daniel Henry Kahnweiler.* Three volumes. Scheduled for publication 2015-6.

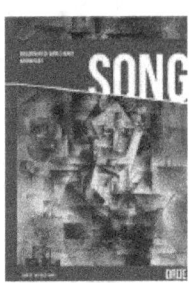

Conversations and interviews

11   *orde's Conversations with Henry Moore.* Henry Moore talks about influences, the artists he likes, his work and life in general. Available as eBook 2013 Book published by Song 2014

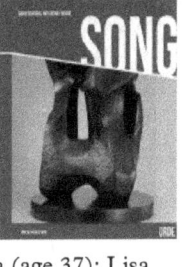

12   *Orde's Conversations with Richard Sorabji (videoed)* in progress,. Richard Sorabji in thought and in person is brought to us in a unique experiment where orde has selected friends from each decade to converse with him. Completed to date are Louis Hynes (age 10); Laurence Hutton-Smith (age 20); Richard Kuziara (age 37); Lisa Hammond-Marty (age 40-50); Jeremy Rowe (age 50-58); Marianne Talbot (age 58--68) Joanna Foster (age 68-80). Available as video, eBook and book. Scheduled publication 2015.

13   *Talking to Solly Irwin (videoed)*
     Schedule publication as eBook and book 2014-5,

Films

14 *Essences.* Independent production produced by orde under the inspiration of Straub and Huillet. A contemplative mood piece starring Richard E. Grant and Kiki Savejan
Director/script/editor: orde
Cast: Richard E Grant, Kiki Savejan
Running Time: 40 minutes/colour
Date Completed: 1983
(Image: Scene Shot from Essences by orde.)

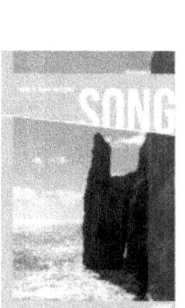

15 Ÿ
Director/script/editor: orde
Cast: Richard E Grant
Running time:16 minutes/colour
Date Completed: c.1987.

Film scripts

16 *The Judgment of Shylock.* In progress.

In fermentation/digestion

17 *The Inventors dilemma.* A novel?
18 *Five Fingers are not the same.* A novel?
19 *Turquoise.* A love story.
20 *The Weather of myself.* A philosophical book/diary.
21 *The Human Tragedy.* A true story, novel/poem?

Music

22 *I am here thank you please, a musical composition.* Contains an introduction on classical and romantic by orde.
Available 2014 as eBook and book (published by Song.

23 *Le Bordel Philosophique.* A musical composition with 5 contemporary composers (George

Barton, Sam Fernando, Cheryl Francis-Hoad, Simon Roth, Jaime Wolfson). A composition based on a poem, which is based on a painting to reach a musical gesamtkunstwerk for our era. Scheduled for completion 2014.

Plays

24   *Forcible Love.* A play based on the life of John Muafangejo.

25   *Forcible Love (NTN version).* A musical on the life of John Muafangejo - premiered at the National Theatre, Windhoek, Namibia for the Independence Celebrations. Includes reviews. Available 2014 as eBook and book (published by Song)

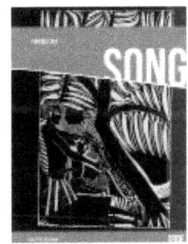

26   *The Rialto Dialogues.* Described as a revolutionary work about the Merchant of Venice by William Shakespeare. It includes the entire work uncut but introduces 4 new characters to open a meaning and channel to one of Shakespeare's greatest plays. Available 2014 as eBook and book (published by Song)

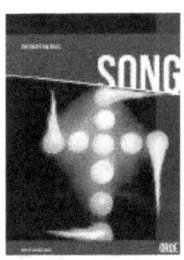

27   *Shylock the Magnificent.* A play 13 years after the Trial Scene of the Merchant of Venice by Shakespeare. Available 2014 as eBook and book (published by Song) See also The Soul's Heritage under poems.

Poems

28   *Miscellaneous poems.* Short poems found over the years. Available 2014 as eBook and book.

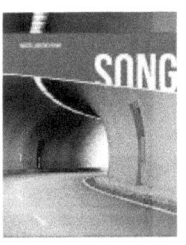

29   *The Love song of D. Adolph Hitler.* In progress.
30   *Der Tod Des Miguel.* In progress

31   *Les Dem.* About Picasso's painting *Les Demoiselles D'Avignon,* includes essay on *Les Dem* by Professor Andrew Laird. Available 2014 as eBook and book (published by Song).

32   *Ndilapa Nkosi.* A lyrical comedy, first part of *The Soul's Heritage*, a trilogy, a landmark work described by Samuel Beckett as a 'moving feat'. Includes reviews and responses from various persons including Beckett.
Available 2014 as eBook and book (published by Song).

33   *Antomat Diplony of the Orb.* An epic comedy, in progress, second part of The Soul's Heritage, a trilogy.

34   *The Argonauta Vineyard.* A tragic comedy, in progress, third part of The Soul's Heritage, a trilogy.

35   *Parlez à Voir.*
Available 2014 as eBook and book (published by Song).

36   *Flying strongly on one wing.*
Available 2014 as eBook and book (published by Song).

37   *Snowflakes and Ashes.*
Available 2014 as eBook and book (published by Song).

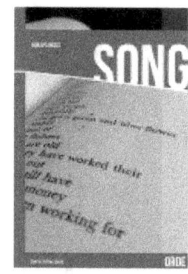

Reviews and articles

38   A number of articles and reviews exist and are being collated.

39   *Art, An Adaptive Function?*
Encyclopaedia of Evolution Mark Pagel (Editor-in-Chief), Oxford University Press, 2002. (365 articles from 330 different authors).

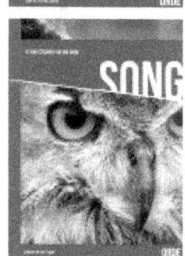

Visual works

   Drawings, paintings, photography, prints, sculptures
Please see www.orde.info

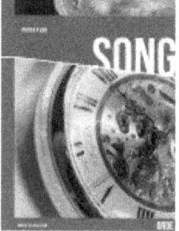

www.ingramcontent.com/pod-product-compliance
Lightning Source LLC
Chambersburg PA
CBHW071231220526
45468CB00002B/808